PROPHECY AND THE PROPHETS

PROPHECY AND THE PROPHETS
IN ANCIENT ISRAEL

THEODORE H. ROBINSON

THIRD EDITION

with a new bibliography by

G. W. ANDERSON, F.B.A.

Professor of Hebrew and Old Testament Studies
University of Edinburgh

DUCKWORTH

First published 1923
Seventh Impression 1948
Eighth Impression, with corrections, 1950
Ninth Impression with new bibliography, 1979

Gerald Duckworth & Co Ltd
The Old Piano Factory
43 Gloucester Crescent
London NW1

© 1979 by Gerald Duckworth & Co Ltd
ISBN 0 7156

Printed by A. Wheaton & Co. Ltd, Exeter

οὐ γὰρ θελήματι ἀνθρώπου ἠνέχθη προφητεία ποτέ, ἀλλὰ ὑπὸ
Πνεύματος Ἁγίου φερόμενοι ἐλάλησαν ἀπὸ Θεοῦ ἄνθρωποι.

II. Pet. i. 21,

ἵνα γένηται ἐν πᾶσιν αὐτὸς πρωτεύων.

Col. i. 18.

CONTENTS

PREFACE

THERE are few branches of Biblical study in which greater advance has been made in the last thirty years than the prophetic literature. The whole subject of prophetic psychology has been under investigation, and whilst it would be too early to say that the conclusions reached in the following pages are final, it may be claimed that they do fairly represent the trend of present-day thought. At the same time they are as yet hardly available for the English reader, being for the most part interred in scattered magazine articles—those lonely graves which few but the most determined and enthusiastic specialists care to rifle. Perhaps the only book which gives due place to them is Dr. Skinner's new work on Jeremiah, *Prophecy and Religion*.

It is my hope to be able in the following pages to bring before the general English reader a position which is being more and more fully accepted in this country. It is true that it is still far from being universally held, and some of the greatest of British Old Testament scholars still deny that there was any ecstatic element in the life of the canonical prophets. The reader will be able to form his own judgment on the basis of the material supplied and suggested in the present volume.

I have at the same time tried to indicate, in dealing with each individual prophet, the part he played in the development of the religion of Israel. I have made no attempt to give a complete study of the work of any of

PREFACE

them, and where the book is likely to be well known I have deliberately refrained from repeating much that is familiar. I have therefore aimed at trying to set the prophets in their true place in the story of the revelation of God to man. To a Christian writer there can be only one centre—Christ. The Old Testament is the record of the preparation for His coming, and the supreme service that the modern study of the Bible has done is that its rearrangement of the material has shewn us the steps and the methods of God in that preparation. It is my hope that my work, slight as it is, may help the Christian public to a fuller understanding of that amazing, continuous, and progressive miracle exhibited in the spiritual history of Israel.

There remains to me the very pleasant duty of acknowledging the help I have received in the preparation of this volume from many friends. Three well-known Old Testament Scholars, in particular, have rendered services which demand special mention. The Rev. Canon G. H. Box and Prof. A. S. Peake were good enough to read the work in typescript, and to make a number of useful comments. Dr. Peake also interested himself in the Bibliography which will be found at the end, and it is due largely to his kindness that I am able to claim that the student will find mentioned there practically all the more important modern literature of the subject. Finally the Rev. Principal H. Wheeler Robinson was good enough to read the whole in proof, to call my attention to many slips, ambiguities, and other weaknesses in expression. Whilst these gentlemen have freely offered material suggestions of value, they have all been generous enough not to insist on their own views, and I must accept for myself the full responsibility for any erroneous opinions or statements which the reader may find

THEODORE H. ROBINSON.

CARDIFF,
 February, 1923.

Prophecy and the Prophets

I

ANCIENT SEMITIC RELIGION

WHY was Jesus a Jew ? God has never left Himself
without witness, and as far as it has been possible to
study the life and thought of humanity, it has always
appeared that men have had some knowledge of Him, or
at least some knowledge and faith which may lead up to
Him. Jesus is the supreme revelation of God to man, but
wherever His messengers have gone to try to bring Him
to men, they have found in the belief of those amongst
whom they worked, something which they could use as a
basis for their teaching, some starting point from which they
could lead men towards Christ. This has been true from
the age of the first missionary effort of the Christian
Church ; it is true of the world-wide evangelism of to-day.
Just as Paul could argue from that which he had in common
with his hearers in every place, so the modern missionary
can find everywhere a ground of appeal in the very creed
which he seeks to supplant. The stress is not to-day on
the utter falsity of the non-Christian religions of the world,
but on their incompleteness. That there is much in them
which a more perfect knowledge of God would and does
discard is only too obvious to those who have been in
contact with them, but it is equally obvious that there is
hardly any cardinal doctrine of the Christian faith which

has not been perceived, however dimly, by men in other ages and of other creeds.

It is equally true that no great race has ever entered the Christian Church without contributing materially to its knowledge of God in Christ. That is why Greek Christianity was a different thing from Roman, and why again, when the Teutonic nations of northern Europe came to express Christ for themselves (and that is the true meaning of the Reformation), they had to break away from the older Church and think out their position afresh. And every form of Christianity to-day owes much to Greek thought, and possibly much (though this is still a matter of dispute) to various types of oriental religion which were current in the Græco-Roman world into which Christ came.

The Jew was a person of no political importance and of no social standing. He was almost as unpopular in the Roman world as he is in Eastern Europe to-day, though not equally persecuted. He inhabited a little strip of land between the Mediterranean and the Syrian desert, and for six centuries had only intermittently enjoyed an approximate national independence. He was to the fore in commerce then as now—he had little else to live for besides his faith—but political influence was almost denied him, and political dominance was a dream which appeared even to those who dreamed it to demand a more amazing divine interference with humanity than the world had ever witnessed. Yet Jesus was a Jew and not a Roman.

Nor was it to the Jew that men turned for the leadership of thought. That was the special province and privilege of Greece, whose philosophy not merely dominated the mind of the ancient world, but stamped its phraseology—and far more than its phraseology—on all the later thinking of Christian Europe. The Jew was a person of concrete mind. That idealism in philosophy which has shewn itself to be indispensable to Christianity manifested itself in him only when he learnt it from Greece. Whilst it is true that the channel by which some at least of the great ideas of the Greek came into the Christian mind was a Jewish one—Philo—it is equally true that Philo himself could never have had a message for the world had he not sat at other feet than those of the Jewish Rabbis. Christianity—that revelation of God which Jesus came to bring—offers the highest idealism that the world has ever seen. The Jew was almost incapable of idealistic thinking. Yet Jesus was a Jew and not a Greek.

Judaism has not always been a conspicuously missionary religion.[1] Its adherents have grown in numbers through the ages, yet rather from within, by natural increase, than by the accretion of converts from without. This has been due in part to the persecutions which have beset the Jew but not wholly so, and even where the Jew has had a free hand to proselytise if he would, he has preferred to keep himself to himself, and leave the Gentile to go his own way. There has been a trickle of foreign converts into the Jewish Church, it is true, but in the main the great challenge to the spiritual empire of the world flung out by the writer of Isaiah lx. and the Book of Jonah has remained unheeded, and the propagation of the faith of the Jewish Scriptures themselves has been left to Christian and Gentile peoples. The great missionary races of the world have been the Arabian and the Indian. It was in the country of the latter that Buddhism had its rise, and though the faith has been dead these many centuries in the land of its birth, it is the creed which to-day claims more adherents than any other. And the typical Arab faith has passed far beyond its original borders, and now spreads in a great belt over the northern tropical and sub-tropical portions of the Old World. It is true that the

---

[1] The great exception seems to have been in the last three centuries B.C., when the Jews of the Diaspora did win numbers of men and women from heathenism. *Cf.* G. H. Box on *Judaism and Hellenism,* in the *Church Quarterly Review* for October, 1922.

method of its extension was in early days mainly that of
violence, but this was not the case with the gentle mission-
aries of Buddhism, who followed that course which has
always been held up as the ideal one for spreading a religion.
Yet Jesus was neither Arab nor Indian : He was a Jew.

Clearly there were elements in Judaism which were to
be found nowhere else, which were absolutely indispensable
as a basis for the revelation of God in Christ. They are to
be sought not so much in the teaching of Jesus as in His
assumptions—less in the things that He said than in the
things He did not say. This is immediately apparent when
one compares the teaching and language of Jesus with that
of Paul, especially when the latter is writing to Christians
who have come direct from the ordinary Gentile heathenism.
There the reader feels that the Apostle is facing problems
with which Jesus never dealt, except by implication.

Paul is face to face with idolatry and heathenism, often
of the grossest kind. Those whom he sought to win dwelt
in an atmosphere of " lords many and gods many." The
cities in which he preached were rich in temples, and their
worship affected the ordinary affairs of every day life. The
very food to be purchased in the open market was all the
cheaper if it had passed through the hands of some heathen
priest. The existence of the gods and goddesses in whose
honour the temples had been erected might be denied, and
the figures which represented them condemned as mere
wood and stone with no spiritual being behind them. Or
the reality of the deities might be admitted whilst they
were classed with demons and devils as powers of darkness.
But, real or unreal, their influence and worship had to be
taken into account, and formed the big problem of the
early Gentile Church.

Jesus, on the other hand, never mentioned them, as far
as we know. His ministrations were mainly confined
to His own people. In dealing with them He was able
to assume a belief in one living and true God, Maker

of heaven and earth and Father of all mankind. Wide as was the gulf which separated Him from some of His compatriots, here He was fully at one with them all. And it is obvious that His teaching would have been meaningless on any other basis. He could not have taught the universal Fatherhood of God if there had been more than One. He could not have proclaimed the Kingdom of God if that sovereignty had been divided between a number of deities. A kingdom, to the oriental mind, must always be a monarchical despotism. There can be no appreciation of the work of Jesus which does not imply a reconciliation between the human and the Divine. You cannot be " reconciled " at one and the same time with a hundred jealous and warring gods and godlings. Given a monotheistic doctrine of God, the teaching of Jesus becomes possible and His work intelligible. Apart from that doctrine, both would be absurd. And Judaism was the only religion in the world with a genuine monotheistic basis. Nowhere else could Jesus have assumed that position which was the very foundation of all He had to say and do.

Further, paradoxical as it seems to-day, the ancient world saw no necessary connection between religion and morality. The gods and goddesses were magnified human beings, with human virtues and human vices, but without the restraints which conscience and society impose on men. In so far as they became specialised in character, some were held to be good, and their worship had ethical elements, but others were equally held to be wicked As in modern Hinduism, so in the religions of the ancient world, there was hardly a vice or crime which could not be committed, not merely with the connivance, but with the sanction and even direct authority of one or other of the world's numerous deities. So complete was the divorce between religion and morality that not a few of the great souls of the ancient world discarded the gods altogether for practical purposes, and took refuge in an atheistic philosophy. To them religion and righteousness were incompatible, and they preferred to follow the light of their own conscience.

Jesus never had to insist that God was good. It was assumed, both by Himself and by those who were about Him. He not infrequently had to point men to a higher standard of goodness than that which they had hitherto held, but this did not affect the essential similarity between His position and theirs. His whole conception of religion was based on a *moral* God. In conduct He bade men be perfect, as their heavenly Father was perfect. All Christian teaching on redemption has recognised it as resulting in a moral union between the human and the divine, and though the teaching has often been crude and even casuistic, that insistence on goodness has been a constant feature.

There are wide differences in belief and in outlook between Judaism and Christianity. Yet this two-sided doctrine of an ethical monotheism is fundamental to both, and (if we except the far lower moral standard of Islam—itself based on Judaism) peculiar to both. When Jesus came into the world the Jew stood on a lonely pinnacle of faith, untouched and indeed unapproached by any other creed. For that reason, it would seem, the supreme revelation of God could come only in Israel ; Jesus was of necessity a Jew.

But whilst Judaism thus reached a unique point in the history of the world's religion, it started on the same level as most early forms of human faith, especially as it appeared amongst kindred peoples. When we first meet with the Hebrews, their religion, life and belief seem to be hardly distinguishable from those of the nations who were round about them. Moabite, Edomite, Ammonite, Canaanite, Phœnician, Syrian, all springing from a common stock, face the world with similar or at least parallel conceptions of God and of His relation to man. The great miracle of Judaism is to be found, not in a peculiar origin but in a unique development.

The Hebrews belonged to that branch of the human race to which we usually give the name Semitic. The Semites form a distinct and well-defined group of peoples, clearly marked off from the rest of mankind in language and in physical characteristics. In addition to the peoples just mentioned, the group includes also the inhabitants of Arabia and a certain element in the population of Mesopotamia. The early Semite lived in a world peopled by personal beings, of whom the human race formed only one species. To his imagination even the animals, wild or domestic, were personal. Further, every natural object might conceal within itself some spirit. Mountains, rivers, trees, springs, or stones might at any moment be revealed as the homes of beings who were like man in possessing personality, though they differed from him in other respects. Experience led men to class them in different groups, some as hostile, some as friendly, others possibly as indifferent, but all as possessed of powers denied to man. In certain instances their attitude was determined by their direct relation to one or other of the groups to which men belonged.

The social organisation of the ancient Israelites and of their neighbours was essentially tribal. That is to say, every man belonged to a natural community, and the members of each such community were bound to one another by ties of kinship and common blood. Normally all would claim descent from the same ancestor, and if a stranger were admitted, the ceremony of initiation would include rites which implied a fictitious blood-relationship. In addition to the human members of the tribe, the animals were in some way included, though it is clear that their personality was quite different from that of the men and women. Above all, each tribe included at least one god or goddess.

In later times, it is true, gods and goddesses multiplied with the people, and might be built up into an ordered family or Pantheon. This happened in the case of Greece and Rome, and also in Babylonia, where the conquest and absorption of numbers of cities by a central power brought the various gods and goddesses into relation with one another. In the desert, the country occupied by the flocks of the pastoral tribes, this process of conquest and absorption was much less common, and to a great extent the rule " one god one tribe, one tribe one god " seems to have been observed. Thus the Ammonites included amongst their members the god Moloch, the Moabites included the god Chemosh, and the Syrians of Damascus the god Hadad or Rimmon.

It was inevitable that the god should be by far the greatest person in the tribe. He was invisible and immortal, and these two qualities gave him power and authority over all who came into relations with him. He could, if he so chose, make himself visible to men, and did so when it was necessary to make a special revelation to them. If, for instance, he wished them to know that he was living in a new spot, he would prove the fact by causing someone to be directly conscious of his presence. This is in part the meaning of the dream of Jacob at Bethel, and of the appearance of the Burning Bush to Moses ; but there are other instances in the Old Testament in which a holy place derived its sanctity from some similar revelation. The god was thus thought of as having one or more homes, but he was able at the same time to travel with his own tribe. As a member of that tribe he shared in its fortunes, fought its battles, and directed its course. The symbols of his presence might even be carried with the warriors in time of war, and victory was always attributed to his intervention. It would seem that the tribe never admitted the defeat of its god ; if they themselves were worsted by their enemies, they attributed the disaster to his anger, not to his weakness. Amongst his own tribe, the god had special rights and responsibilities, particularly those of deciding disputes between its members. His position there was that of a king, a general, and a judge, and as far as his people were concerned his will was absolute.

The god might be approached in various ways. Prayer, if rightly offered, would secure his attention. A night spent at a shrine might bring a dream, or other revelation, from the god ; but the normal method of communion was sacrifice. Sacrifice in the first instance was probably a common meal. All members of the tribe, human and divine, met together to cement their relationship by sharing in the flesh of one of the tribal animals, which partook of the common life. It is a noteworthy fact that down to a late period in the history of Israel, the flesh of the domestic or tribal animals could only be eaten with the ritual of communion or sacrifice. But sacrifice, whilst it renewed the actual communion between the god and his tribe, could not fulfil all demands. Men needed to approach the god on personal matters. They required from time to time direct expressions of his will. Gods were peculiar people, capricious in their demands, and " faddy " in their ways. Thus the personal approach to a god might be dangerous unless it was made by, or through, some skilled person. Such persons were Priests. Their first duty was the care of the shrine, or any objects with which the tribal god was particularly associated. Their services in this direction gave them a closer acquaintance with the god himself, and enabled them to give safe advice to worshippers, or, in their place, to carry out the desirable rites. Such persons were especially necessary because a dissatisfied god was one of the worst dangers to which humanity was exposed. If a god lost his tribe through the defeat or death of all its members, he continued to exist, but as a source of peril, to all human beings. He was something like a " rogue " elephant, but far more dangerous. Instead of belonging to a civilised community he was wild. The Jinn of Arab mythology seem to have been originally such " wild gods " who, having lost their tribes—or perhaps never having had tribes—were lonely, savage and cruel, with their hand against every man. A good instance of this danger appears when Northern Israel was carried away into captivity. The " mixed peoples " who took their place brought their own gods with them. The God of Israel was neglected, and took His revenge by plaguing men with lions. The danger was only overcome when Priests were fetched back from captivity to instruct the new settlers in the worship of the God of the land.[1]

It may be taken for granted that there was always a sacred object of some kind which was in a special sense associated with the tribal god. The commonest in Palestine, at any rate, seem to have been plain natural pillars. Some of these were stones set on end, others were wooden, almost certainly the trunks of trees. In other cases, especially those of wandering pastoral tribes, smaller and more portable objects served the purpose. Sometimes they would be rude figures, human or animal. The " silver gods " made by Micah[2] seem to have been of this type, for they were easily removed by the Danites. Natural objects, such as stones, might also be used for a similar purpose. These things were held to be not merely sacred to the god, but to contain his very presence. They were naturally under the guardianship of the Priests, and it was to them that sacrificial offerings were made. When a victim was killed, its blood would be poured on the object or on the ground beneath it. From time to time an offering of oil or some other desirable liquid would be poured over it. In any case it possessed the full sanctity of the god himself.

From this very brief sketch it will be realised that the religion of the early Semites was of the most primitive type. It was, in fact, only a stage higher than fetichism,

---

[1] II Kings xvii. 24-28.
[2] Jud. xvii. 1-5.

and there are even hints of totemism, particularly in the animal names borne by men and women, which were more common in early times than in later days.   But, as Robertson Smith remarks of pre-Mohammedan Arabia, the early Semites were very primitive, and often must be regarded as mere savages.   It is not strange that their religion should correspond to their social and intellectual development, nor would it have been surprising if that faith had grown along lines familiar almost everywhere else—Greece, Rome, Egypt, Babylonia, India, and other places.   The fact that is surprising, the real miracle, lies in the growth of the religion of Israel into that unique phenomenon which it was when Jesus came.

II

THE TWO RELIGIONS OF ISRAEL

WHILST there seems thus to have been a common element in the religions of the early Semitic peoples, there were necessarily differences which corresponded to the various grades of civilisation reached by different peoples and tribes. We may broadly distinguish three types—the pastoral, the agricultural, and what we may call (though somewhat inaccurately) the imperial. Each of these belongs to a separate stage in the evolution of human society. The first is that of the independent nomadic tribe, whose wealth consists purely of animals, such as sheep, goats, and camels. The second is characteristic of the settled tribe, which in the main retains its unity and distinctness, having hardly risen to the position of a city state, though it is localised and tied down by its agricultural operations to a comparatively small area. The third appears when several such small tribes unite, either by agreement or conquest, to form a single large state in which all the members more or less fully adopt one another's gods, though doubtless, a god has higher honour in the city which was originally his own. Amongst Semitic races an example of the first may be seen in pre-Mohammedan Arabia, of the second in Canaan before the Hebrew conquest, and of the third in historic Babylonia. It may be remarked at once that whilst it is necessary to include this third stage in order to have a complete conspectus of the normal evolution of religion, it does not enter, save by way of contrast, into a discussion of Hebrew faith.

When we first meet with the Hebrews, they are still in the nomadic or pastoral stage. Their great liberator and leader, Moses, had not merely rescued them—or some of them—from Egypt. but had united the various tribes into a single nation by consecrating them to a single God. This was Yahweh[1], whose home was at Sinai or Horeb. The former seems to have been not far from Kadesh Barnea (the traditional site in the Sinai peninsula is now generally discarded), and the latter in the neighbourhood of the northern end of the Gulf of Akabah, the eastern arm of the Red Sea. The discrepancy as to the place does not affect the historicity of the events, and we may safely look back to Moses as the founder of Israel, both in politics and in religion. But it is fairly clear that the Law in its present form is adapted to an agricultural rather than a pastoral life. Probably we know little in detail of the religion of Israel in the desert.

Some things, however, are perfectly clear. One is that

---

[1] It is probably unnecessary to remark that this name has been disguised in our English versions. For fear of taking the name in vain, the Jews always refused to pronounce it at all, even in reading the Scriptures, and wherever it occurred used instead the word " 'adonay," which means " Lord." Hebrew in ancient times was written with consonants only ; the vowel signs were invented when the language ceased to be spoken. The text was held to be too sacred for any alteration, so the scribes kept the consonants YHWH, but inserted the vowels of 'adonay, i.e. A (a very short indistinct vowel), O and A. From this mixed form the hybrid word Yehovah or Jehovah arose. The early versions—Greek, Syriac, and Latin—carried the scruples of the Rabbis so far that they translated "'adonay," not "Yahweh," writing always the word for " Lord." They have been followed by the English translators, who, however, indicated the proper name by using capitals. Hence the reader of the Old Testament should always remember that when the word LORD occurs, it represents the personal name of Yahweh, which actually stands in the Hebrew text.

which has already been mentioned, the association of the
nation with Yahweh. " I will become their God and they
shall become my people " is the formula of adoption, the
principle of " Covenant," which persisted all through the
history of Israel. It was the foundation on which the whole
of the later edifice was erected. In pursuance of this
Covenant, Yahweh was the guide of the people through the
desert, leading them by safe paths and finding herbage for
their flocks. When enemies appeared, He was in the midst
of His people, fighting their battles. One of His titles is " God
of Armies," originally, we may suppose, the armies of
Israel. Within the tribe He exercised all judicial functions,
and to Him, or rather to His Priests, men brought disputes
for settlement. He entered into every department of
tribal life. Again and again it seemed as though the bond
might weaken and even break, but it did in fact hold until
Yahweh's people were ready to learn that He was not as
the gods of other nations.

Further details, however, are uncertain and obscure.
Whilst recognising that Yahweh's home was in the mountain
where they had first met Him, the nomadic Hebrews carried
with them portable symbols in the form of stones. These
had been received—so their tradition ran, and there is no
reason to doubt it—at the mountain, and were a concrete
sign of the Covenant. They were kept in a closed box, and
this remained the most sacred object in Israel right down to
the destruction of the Temple in 586 B.C. It also seems
certain that the guardianship of the box and its contents
was in the hands of Moses and the family to which he
belonged. It had, needless to say, a tent of its own, and
that tent was the natural meeting-place for God and man.
From this tent the sacred emblems would be taken in time
of war to lead the armed men into battle, when it was
supposed that Yahweh would strike the enemy with panic.
It is also possible that from time to time it would be
employed to indicate the route the tribe should take. It

was certainly credited with the power of controlling draught animals and of choosing its own road.[1]

Our earliest testimony—that of the eighth and seventh century Prophets—is unanimous in disputing the Divine ordinance of sacrifice in the wilderness.[2] Nor can we suppose that the seasonal feasts were observed before the conquest of Canaan. It is a significant fact that even in the earliest piece of ritual legislation that has come down to us, the decalogue which forms the core of Ex. xxxiv,[3] the festivals are nearly all of an agricultural character, and could have been observed only by a people settled on the land and tilling the soil year after year. An exception must be made in the case of the Passover. It is worth noting that the oldest reference (again Ex. xxxiv.) does not regard the Passover merely as a sacrifice (Hebrew *zebah* or *ʿolah*), but as a " festival " (Hebrew *hag*), a word which is still used amongst the Arabian tribes of a pilgrimage. It will be remembered that the plea on which Moses claimed liberty for Israel was that she needed to observe a " festival " to her God,[4] whom she evidently did not know very well,[5] and because she was unable to reach the sacred spot in time she observed the ceremonial in Egypt. It is thus open to us to conjecture that the Passover was, during the nomadic period at any rate, an annual festival celebrated, not at any chance encampment on the route, but at the sacred mountain, towards which the tribes would move at the appointed season.

We have thus a picture, vague and indistinct it is true, but yet of sufficient clearness to show us an extraordinary

---

[1] *Cf.* I Sam. vi. 12, where the lowing of the oxen is especially mentioned to shew that they took the road they did under protest. They were being driven against their will by the Power residing in the Ark.
[2] Amos implies that it did not exist, v. 25 ; Jeremiah states that it was not due to Yahweh's command, vii. 22. There are frequent statements of the futility of sacrifice in the Prophet's own day, *cf.* Is. i, 11. Jer. vi. 20, Hos. iv. 13, v. 6, viii. 11, Am. iv. 4., Mi. vi. 6-8.
[3] *Cf.* H. P. Smith, *Religion of Israel*, p. 110 f. [4] Ex. v. 1, x. 9, etc.
[5] Ex. x. 26.

simplicity of worship. There is practically no ritual, and we miss all the paraphernalia of external religion. At the same time nomadic peoples commonly have a fairly high ethical standard.[1] Their sexual morality is comparatively pure (the modern gypsy is a case in point). Private property hardly exists, and they are thus saved from many of the moral and social perils which beset men on a higher plane of civilisation. Moreover, in view of His judicial functions, as the supreme arbiter in all cases of dispute between members of the tribe, Yahweh became inevitably the guardian of their simple but comparatively pure ethics. There is no reason to doubt that the moral (as distinct from the religious) element in the decalogue of Ex. xx. fairly represents the standard of life which Yahweh required of His people in the desert.

Over against this primitive faith and society we have the Canaanite civilisation. The Canaanites had come originally from the same general Semitic stock as the Hebrews, had settled on the land in pre-historic times, and were largely an agricultural people. They had, however, retained an organisation similar to that of the desert tribes, though each group was necessarily limited by geographical bounds. They had never attained to a genuine unity, nor is there any historical evidence to show that one tribe or city ever succeeded in subduing or in dominating its neighbours. Palestine has always been the bridge between Asia and Africa, and this fact, combined with the isolation of each township or petty state, made them an easy prey to one or other of the great world powers. At some early stage the country was clearly overrun by the great Hittite race, whose retreating tide left not a few pools behind it. Even in late times we find colonies or groups of Hittites, far

[1] Persons acquainted both with southern and central Africa assure me that the moral standard of the Zulu, who is a nomad, is a good deal higher than that of the agricultural natives of the Congo, though their religious beliefs and practices are on much the same level

removed from the historic centre of their empire in the north, still maintaining an independent existence amongst their Semitic neighbours. In the middle of the third millennium B.C. the dominant influence was that of Babylon, whose first empire reached its zenith under Hammurabi. It was probably during this period that the traditions, mythology, and civil law of Babylon impressed themselves on the Canaanites. For it is clear that their civilisation was Babylonian rather than Hittite or Egyptian, and when, a thousand years later, the little Palestinian states owned allegiance to the Egyptian court, the official correspondence was carried on neither in the language of Egypt nor in that of Canaan, but in that of Babylon. There were, of course, long intervals during which no effective control was exercised by any outside power, and the various states were left to quarrel amongst themselves or to fall a prey to wilder but stronger marauding tribes from the desert.

The religion of these settled Semites naturally developed to suit the conditions of an agricultural community. The tribal god became the local god. He does not always seem to have a name of his own, but is indicated by the general term " Baal." This is a word which means both " owner " and " husband," and its correlatives are " slave " and " wife." Thus the Baal of any particular place is the master of the people and the husband of the land. Every village and town had its shrine or " high place," situated either on a neighbouring hill-top or under some conspicuous tree. There might be substantial buildings, as at the recently excavated site of Gezer ; but in any case there would be the divine symbols—an upright stone or a wooden post, frequently both.[1] Sometimes other symbols would appear, and Baals seem to have been worshipped under the forms of the bull and of the snake. No doubt some of their

---

[1] *Cf*. Jud. vi. 28, where the " altar " of Baal is probably the sacred pillar or " massebah."

sanctuaries were more famous than others, and might be visited by members of other communities.

The religion of an agricultural community tends towards nature worship in some form or other. The Baals, as their very name implies, were gods of fertility. The sexual idea was carried to a practical extreme, with the result that there appeared in the worship of Canaan the revolting practice of ritual fornication. Sacrifice also was offered. Sometimes it would be the more primitive kind, the common meal in which worshipper, priest, and god all shared. But for special purposes and on special occasions a second type was employed, the " burnt-offering " or " whole burnt-offering." In this case the sacrifice was a gift to the god, and the worshipper ate no part of it, though possibly in some instances the Priest might take a share. First fruits, both of animals and of vegetable products, were classed under this head, and the victims at times included even human beings—possibly first-born infants.

Special festivals were connected as a rule with the seasons. It seems likely that there were particular ceremonies and offerings made at the beginning and end of the corn harvest and at the end of the vintage. There appears also to have been a lunar festival, taken from Babylon in the first instance, held at each quarter of the moon—that is, weekly. These were probably occasions of licence and even riotousness. We may be fairly sure, for instance, that the festival of the grape harvest involved a copious use of wine. Such occasions were opportunities for relief from the grim and relentless toil which forms the normal lot of the agricultural worker, and the general result was that some of the restraints of everyday conduct were discarded. So it came to pass that men found in their religion a gratification of passions which, under normal conditions, civil and social morality required them to control.

Apart from their religion it would seem that the morality of the Canaanites was much on the same level as that of other nations. We have no direct evidence as to the type of civil law current amongst them, but the probability is that it conformed to the Babylonian standard. That is recorded for us in the famous " Code of Hammurabi," and in the absence of other evidence we are justified in supposing that its principles were accepted wherever Babylonian influence reached. But it seems clear that the ethic, though good as far as it went, was in effect " case-law," and when conditions arose which were not considered or contemplated in the current systems of law, men followed their own inclination rather than any guiding principle. This would happen particularly when cities of any size sprang up or as a commercial life developed in the country. One thing is clear. Apart from such a limited system of details the Canaanite religion gave little or no help towards the moral life. No doubt if a man swore by a Baal, that Baal would see to it that he kept his word or suffered for it. But this was not due to the god's sense of the inherent value of truthfulness, but rather to his own objection to being personally slighted. He would equally take vengeance for the violation of other rules—such, perhaps, as stepping on the threshold of his shrine—which carried no moral content with them at all. And the graver social sins— greed, oppression, legal corruption, cheating and the like— met with no punishment at his hands.

Whilst, of course, the Priests continued to be the most prominent and regular of the religious officials, it is clear that they were no longer the only such class of persons. Baals do not seem to have been jealous as long as they received their due. For one thing they were in a measure tied to the soil, and their authority did not extend beyond the frontiers of their city or tribe. There were other unofficial spiritual beings who were consulted if not worshipped. Some of these may have been the gods of dispossessed or destroyed tribes—the " Jinn " of Arab theology. Others were the ghosts of the departed, for the dead in their subterranean home were still supposed to be within reach of those who had the proper knowledge. Dealings with these classes were in the hands of special experts—" diviners," " wizards," " sorcerers," " necromancers "—any or all of whom might be employed in securing a knowledge of the past or of the future. They bore much the same relation to the " unofficial " spirits as the Priests did to the official Baals.

Other persons were more closely connected with the tribal deity. There were men who devoted themselves to the service of the god without being definitely attached to the shrine. Some of these had peculiar powers, in particular the gift of " second sight," by which they became conscious of a world other than the normal, and were able to see and hear things hidden from the ordinary man. Such men were " Seers." There were also enthusiasts, some of whom were deliberately self-dedicated to extolling their god, whilst others took up their task under compulsion. The latter were subject to strange seizures, which were attributed to possession by the Baal. Any psychological phenomenon which the East does not understand is explained as being due to a " breathing." That is to say, some being, usually divine, has " breathed " into the person concerned and taken complete control over him. A " breath " or "spirit " has " rushed " upon him, and manifests itself in abnormal behaviour. Generally it was held to be the god who was responsible for the condition, and had produced what we to-day call " ecstasy." A person once seized by this ecstasy becomes liable to it all his life. Though such " Ecstatics " were possibly disliked and despised by the regular priesthood, they were held in reverence by the common people, and form one of the most striking features of the religious life of Canaan.

We have now to consider the effect produced on Israel by their entry into Palestine and their contact with Canaanite civilisation and religion. The conquest was neither sudden nor complete. The first stage left the Hebrews in three main groups—one in the far north, one in the central Ephraimite hills, and one in the far south. Two belts of unsubdued Canaanites separated them from one another. The more northerly of hese lay in the fertile Esdraelon district. The victory of Deborah and Barak[1] did something to weaken the Canaanite power here, and the struggles of Abimelech secured for Israel a permanent footing in the plains. For the rest it would seem that unity was secured by slow assimilation and absorption, a process no doubt accelerated to some extent by the common necessity for meeting Philistine pressure. We may suspect that there was a strong Canaanite element in the blood of the later Israelites of the north. The southern belt had its strongest post in the ancient city of Jerusalem, which did not fall into Israelite hands till the time of David. In early days, the greater part of the period covered by the Book of Judges, it is clear that the Hebrews were confined to the mountains, forests, and wilder parts of the country, making good their footing in the more fertile areas very slowly. Consequently it was only gradually that they undertook agriculture, and became familiar with its processes.

Amongst the more primitive races, religion is inextricably intertwined with men's regular avocations. Israel had known Yahweh as a God of storms, mountains and deserts. He had led them in safety through all natural dangers, and by His military prowess had beaten off all their enemies. They had every reason to be proud of Him, and He had every claim on their loyalty. But it was inevitable that doubts should arise when they entered on the new life symbolised by grain and vine and olive. The Baals were already in possession. If neglected they might become dangerous.[2] But, further, there was the uncertainty as

[1] Jud. iv. and v.
[2] *Cf.* II. Kings xvii. 24-28.

to whether Yahweh could grow corn. Certainly they had had no experience of His abilities in that direction, and we have the direct statement of Hosea to the effect that this doubt lasted in some quarters down to the middle of the eighth century.[1]

In these circumstances it is not surprising that Israel tended to worship the Baals for agricultural purposes. But retribution followed. Disunited, the Hebrews were an easy prey to their stronger and more highly civilised enemies, who defeated, oppressed, and enslaved them. Scattered as they were, they had only one bond of union—Yahweh. It was in His name that deliverers arose and summoned all the tribes to the relief of the suffering clan.[2] Then, and only then, were they victorious ; and it was in the period of the Judges that they began to learn by bitter experience that *unbroken fidelity to Yahweh was essential to their continued national existence*. This was the first great lesson, and the first definite step towards their ultimate spiritual goal.

But, even when men admitted Yahweh to be a God of agriculture, further questions might well arise as to the manner of His worship. It did not follow that because He was the same God whom they had known in earlier days, therefore they ought to worship Him as they had done in the desert. On the contrary, it seemed natural that new rites should be required. Yahweh was now the God of the fertile land—practically a Baal—and would surely require to be honoured as such. The result was the curious religious phenomenon which we call " syncretism," which means the coalescence of two religions, the god or gods of the one being worshipped with the ritual proper to another. It seems that Israel took over almost intact the whole cultus of the Canaanites

---

[1] Hos. ii. 8.
[2] *Cf*. Jud. v. 23, where Meroz is cursed, not for failing to fight for Israel, but for failing to help Yahweh.

and, indeed, far more than the cultus—their language[1] and practically all their civilisation. For our purpose it will be sufficient to notice the following points.

The high places, or old Canaanite sanctuaries, became the sites of Yahweh's worship. True, these were forbidden in the Deuteronomic law, but there seems to be not the slightest objection to them in the days of Samuel, and even Elijah and Amos appear to have made no protest against them as such. There seems to have been no definite regulation of the priesthood, though there is a decided preference for members of the tribe, or perhaps rather class, to which Moses belonged.[2] The sacred objects and emblems remained untouched, at any rate in northern Israel, and in the Pentateuch itself the stone pillar or " massebah " is mentioned with apparent acquiescence. Whilst the stones in their box continued to be the most sacred and characteristic object of worship, Yahweh was represented and revered under two other forms, both probably derived from Canaanite sources. One of these, that employed in the south, was a certain species of snake. It is true that this cult was put down by Hezekiah, but it is significant that Isaiah, in his great Call-vision, sees the attendants of Yahweh in the shape of that particular serpent, the " seraph." In the north Yahweh was worshipped in the likeness of a bull, and till Hosea, no protest is made against this particular element in the Samaritan cultus. Even Amos passes it by in silence.

It seems also clear that the sacrificial rites and formulæ of the high places were retained—including both infant sacrifice and sacramental fornication. No doubt the former

---

[1] That Hebrew was originally the language of Canaan is shewn both by the analogy of other Canaanite dialects and by the Tell-el-Amarna Tablets. In the nomadic period the Israelites probably spoke some form of Aramaic. The name Yahweh itself seems to be Aramaic rather than Hebrew.

[2] *Cf.* Jud. xvii. 13.

tended to disappear fairly early in the history of Israel.
It is a thing against which the human mind so revolts
that it is, sooner or later, neglected or avoided. Its place
is readily taken by a mock sacrifice or by the substitution
of some animal victim. The latter was the course followed
in Israel, and in later times men were permitted—indeed
compelled—to redeem their first-born with the offering of
an animal. But in cases of extreme national danger, when
disaster seemed almost inevitable, the original sacrifice
might be revived.[1] There were also from time to time out-
breaks of religiosity which led men to go the full length of
the practice. The most famous occurred in the reign of
Manasseh, whose name was handed down to the execration
of later generations on this account. But the Temple
prostitutes, both male and female, seem to have been a
constant feature of Israelite worship down to the time of
Josiah.[2]

The Canaanite festivals also held their place in the new
order. The regular lunar holy days were now strictly
observed in honour of Yahweh. The feast which fell at
the beginning of the harvest coincided with the old Passover
of the desert period, and was combined with it. Its principal feature was the exclusion of all leaven from bread,
no doubt originally in order to avoid spiritual contamination.
The Harvest Home festival was observed seven weeks
later, and became the feast of Pentecost. The Vintage
festival marked the close of the agricultural year and,
later, under the name of the Feast of Tabernacles, Judaism
used it to recall the conditions of the nomadic life.[3] Other
festivals were added from time to time, especially by the
post-exilic community ; but these three, together with the
Day of Atonement, remained the great religious occasions.

---

[1] *E.g.*, by Ahaz, II. Kings xvi. 3, possibly in terror of the Syro-Ephraimite
league. It is curious that no condemnation by Isaiah has been
recorded.
[2] *Cf.* II. Kings xxiii. 7.   [3] *Cf.* Lev. xxiii. 39-43.

It seems probable that the civil law of early Israel was also that generally current in Palestine before the conquest. Doubtless it was modified and adapted, purified and ennobled as the faith of Israel grew ; but even in its earliest form (Ex. xx-xxiii.) it is clearly the code of a settled community. Affinities with the Code of Hammurabi have often been pointed out, and though the resemblance may be, and has been, exaggerated, it is sufficiently great to make complete independence practically impossible. Direct borrowing on the part of Israel is out of the question, and the most probable explanation is that the civil law, like so much of the mythology of Israel, owes its Babylonian colour to the mediate influence of the Canaanite civilisation.

We have thus a picture of the life and religion of early agricultural Israel, which it is difficult to distinguish in type and character from those of the Canaanites. There is, of course, the outstanding difference in the name and personality of the God who is worshipped. The simplicity of the nomadic religion and its comparative moral purity are lost. Yahweh is still strict in some matters in which He was strict before, and still demands and receives the whole-hearted allegiance of Israel. But there is no attempt to adapt His principles and character to the new conditions. As far as religion touches them, it is the religion of the Baals under a new name. To all intents and purposes Yahweh has become a Baal.

It should, however, be noted that this syncretism was very unevenly spread over Israel. It reached its height only in the agricultural parts of the country, the richer and more fertile tracts. In the wastes of the south and east the poverty of the soil and the scarcity of water would not permit of crops, except the very poorest. In such districts cattle, large and small, were still the main forms of wealth, and the type of civilisation retained much of its old nomadic character. The temptations of agriculture and commerce were absent. Land was hardly property, perhaps never

private property at all. Flocks of sheep and herds of cattle
ranged over the hills, winning what sustenance they could
from the scanty herbage. Hence alongside of the syncretistic worship of the fertile land and of the cities, we have
a wilder, simpler, purer faith. To some of the men of the
half-desert, Yahweh's true home was still in the far south.
The emblems and shrines might in a measure represent
Him, but one who would really enter into the closest
communion with Him must seek Him, not in Bethel or
Jerusalem or Beersheba, still less at the village sanctuaries,
but in Horeb, the mount of God.[1]

Further, there were the genuine Yahweh enthusiasts.
Some, like the Seer and the Ecstatic, owed their peculiar
character to the Canaanite religion. But though in outward
behaviour the Ecstatic of Yahweh might be indistinguish-
able from the Ecstatic of Baal, he did stand for his God,
and in his wild passion would brook no rival. He would
even go so far, if need be, as to interfere in politics ; and at
least one great revolution in the northern kingdom was
engineered by Ecstatics in the interests of Yahweh against
a Baal imported from Tyre. Their moral standards were
not always high, but they did at least stand for the national
God. As a rule they seem to have made no protest against
the evils in the life of Israel. But there were others who,
in their devotion to Yahweh, clung to the ideal of the desert
life in its entirety. To them Yahweh could never be an
agricultural God. The most conspicuous of these were the
Nazirites and the Rechabites. Grapes do not grow in the
desert, consequently both eschewed the vine and all its
products. The nomad has no razor ; the Nazirite let his
hair grow. The dwellings of the desert are skin or hair-
cloth tents, or rough shacks built of palm fronds ; the
Rechabite would have nothing to do with houses of brick

---

[1] This is obviously true of Elijah ; Amos, however, definitely locates
Yahweh in Jerusalem, *cf.* Am. i. 2, etc.

or stone. Their position as Yahweh enthusiasts is well illustrated by their sympathy with the prophetic revolution which placed Jehu on the throne.[1] Even when the faith of Israel was most deeply contaminated with the religion of the Baals, native and foreign, it was still true that Yahweh had left Him seven thousand in Israel, all the knees that had not bowed to Baal and all the lips that had not kissed him. Amongst these the Nazirite, the Rechabite, and, above all, the Ecstatic, were necessarily included.

[1] *Cf.* II. Kings x. 15ff.

III

THE NᴇBI'IM.

Of the classes of religious persons mentioned at the close of the last chapter, two claim our special attention because of their importance for the development of the religion of Israel. These are the Seer and the Ecstatic. Whilst in later times, even before the middle period of the Hebrew Monarchies, the two classes coalesced with one another, it is clear that they were originally largely independent. They were possessed of different powers and were characterised by different functions and different behaviour. The Ecstatic existed in Canaan long before the Hebrew conquest, and this is probably true of the Seer also. In early Israel, after the conquest, both seem to have been familiar, but, as often happens with that which is familiar, there is rarely any detailed description of them. There is, however, enough to enable us to reconstruct a picture of them, with the help of what we know of similar phenomena elsewhere.

The typical Seer (Hebrew Hozé or Ro'é) is Samuel, as presented to us in I. Sam. ix. 1—x. 16. The story is the familiar one which tells how Saul sets out to look for his father's asses and finds a kingdom. He has with him a servant, and after some days' unsuccessful search they find themselves near Ramah. The servant tells Saul that there

is a " man of God " of good repute there, and suggests
that they apply to him for information. There is one
possible difficulty—have they money to pay his fee ?
Fortunately, the servant has enough with him. They enter
the town and catch Samuel—now called a Seer—on his
way up to the high place, where there is a public sacrifice.
He holds an honourable position in the town, and is able
to offer the strangers a share in the sacrifice. He has been
in communication with Yahweh the day before, and is
able to tell them at once that the lost animals have been
recovered, at the same time giving a hint of Saul's high
destiny. After the sacrificial meal, at which special honour
is paid to the Seer's guests, Samuel offers his visitors the
shelter of his own home. Next morning he starts with them
on their way, and as soon as they are well out of the city,
he anoints Saul. He then describes three signs which will
be fulfilled before Saul reaches his home, in order that he may
be sure of the accuracy of Samuel's statement regarding
the kingdom. As a matter of fact all the signs are fulfilled,
and the last has a permanent bearing on Saul's own life
and personality.

The first feature that strikes us on reading this narrative
is that Samuel is a " man of God." That is explained by
the fact that he is in direct communication with Yahweh.
He is able on occasion to hear Yahweh's voice, and the
characteristic name of Seer makes it clear that his abnormal
experiences are visual as well as auditory. It would seem
that the second sight and second hearing are to some
extent under his own control, for people expect to be able
to go to him with questions for which he can get answers
at will A fee is usually required, though, as a matter of
fact, in this case there is no note of payment being actually
made. This again implies that the Seer is master of his own
powers and can work to order.

His principal function is to describe events, past, present,
or future, which are hidden from the ordinary man.

Although in this particular instance the question is ultimately one of national importance, the general impression conveyed is that such a man is normally approached on private and sometimes trivial matters. Even Saul's kingship has its personal aspect. A Seer is the man to whom one would naturally go to find articles which had been lost.

It is true that the knowledge he has is derived directly from Yahweh, and that Yahweh may be approached at the shrines, but one gathers that, except in the case of disputes, the Priest at the sanctuary was not normally consulted on the smaller personal matters. Such would be brought by preference to the Seer. It is probable, too, that the Priests' method of consultation was to use some form of sacred lot, which would serve to give assent only to one of two stated alternatives, and would not offer spontaneous information.

Other features appear. Samuel holds a high and honourable position in his own town. He is alone, and has none to share his powers and his labours, but he has the respect of all about him. The sacrifice is a civic festival, not a private one. Only thirty are present at it, and the natural assumption is that they were the most prominent people in the place. Yet even amongst them he holds a position of some authority, and is free, not only to invite strangers to participate, but to give such instructions as he sees fit to the persons officiating at the ceremonial meal. Further, his religious position is so clearly established that, although the narrative contains no hint of priestly functions or authority ascribed to him, the whole company wait for their food till he has pronounced a formal blessing on it. The whole picture is one of a sober, dignified, weighty person, standing high in favour with God and in honour with man.

We now turn to the other type. The Hebrew word for Ecstatic is Nabi', plural N^{e}bi'im (E.V. " Prophet "), and

the verb used of ecstatic behaviour is a reflexive form of
the root from which the noun Nabi' comes. We have more
evidence from which to construct this picture than we had
in the case of the Seer, for the ecstasy in religion became
familiar in later days over the whole Mediterranean world.
It consisted of a fit or attack which affected the whole
body. Sometimes the limbs were stimulated to violent
action, and wild leaping and contortions resulted. These
might be more or less rhythmical, and the phenomenon
would present the appearance of a wild and frantic dance.
At other times there was more or less complete constriction
of the muscles, and the condition became almost cataleptic.
The vocal organs were sometimes involved, noises and sounds
were poured out which might be unrecognisable as human
speech. If definite words were uttered they were often
unintelligible. Face and aspect were changed, and to all
outward appearance the Ecstatic " became another man."
An additional feature was insensibility to pain, and the
extravagant activities of the Ecstatic frequently included
violent slashing and cutting of his own body and limbs.

Ecstatics tended to be gregarious, and usually appeared
and acted in bands. This was partly because the ecstasy
was held to be infectious. It will be remembered that at
the close of the narrative in I. Sam. previously referred to,
Saul met a company of N^ebi'im coming down a hill at
Gibeah. The ecstasy fell on him also, and roused the wonder
of all his acquaintances. He was liable to attacks of the
same kind all his life. His first military exploit was due
to the fact that " the breath of God rushed upon him "
(a technical phrase for the access of the ecstasy).[1] The
same spirit in later years became his bane, for the
activity of the spirit was not yet moralised, and the
ravings from which he sought relief through David's music
are described by the verb[2] which denotes ecstatic behaviour.

[1] I. Sam. xi. 6.   [2] I. Sam. xviii. 10.

Once[1] at least his wild actions included the stripping off of all his clothes and lying naked for twenty-four hours. The N^{e}bi'im who are consulted by Ahab[2] appear all together and act practically as one man. The " Prophets " of Baal are four hundred in number and work together.[3]   Usually the manifestations of the mob grew in intensity, until one would stand out from the rest and give a common message, either by symbol or speech, or both.   The case of Zedekiah amongst Ahab's Prophets comes naturally to mind.

Whilst in a number of cases the ecstasy was clearly spontaneous, there were means employed to induce it. One of these was, no doubt, the imitation of the kind of activity to which it led.   Music was frequently used,[4] also possibly drugs of various kinds, including wine in the case of the Baal Prophets.   In some instances it might begin with the fixing of the eyes on a particular object.   Most people are familiar with the dazed, half hypnotic condition that can be produced by continuous staring at the same thing, and in the case of highly-strung or unbalanced minds such a practice would easily lead to a very abnormal psychical state.

In view of all this, it is not surprising to find that the ecstasy was confused with the wilder forms of insanity. The East has always held madness to be a divine visitation, and has regarded the madman as especially possessed by God.   It will be remembered that the Nabi' whose message fired the train of Jehu's revolt was called a raving lunatic.[5] In contrast to the Seer, their social and moral standing was low, as is shown, not merely by the amazement of Saul's friends at his association with such disreputable people, but also by Amos' indignant repudiation of any connection with them.   Yet they were held to be the very mouthpiece of the god who had " breathed " into them, and their

---

[1] I. Sam. xix. 24.   [2] I. Kings. xxii. 5-28.   [3] I. Kings xviii. 20-29
[4] *Cf.* II. Kings iii. 15.   [5] II. Kings ix. 11.

utterances and symbolic acts were regarded as the direct revelation of his will.

By the close of the Roman Republic the phenomena described were familiar throughout the whole of the Mediterranean world, and were associated with a number of different cults. The closest parallels are to be found in Apuleius' description of the wandering priests of Isis, but in several cases the Greek and Italian oracles present striking resemblances, especially where they were connected with Apollo. Readers of classical literature will recall two conspicuous instances—the ravings of Cassandra in the *Agamemnon* and those of the Sibyl at Cumæ in *Æneid VI*. Cassandra, of course, is an Asiatic, and Cumæ was a Phœnician settlement. Even the Delphic priestess seems to have been subject to similar influences, the ecstasy in her case being due to mephitic vapours rising from the ground. Here the god is Apollo again. Possibly the worship of Dionysus involved similar elements. His first seat in Greece was at Thebes—another Phœnician settle- ment. Herodotus expressly states that ecstatic phenomena in his day did not appear in connection with Isis, save amongst Carian immigrants, who thereby, as he says, betrayed their foreign origin. Caria is in Asia Minor. So is Lycia, which seems to have been the original home of Apollo. Whilst Dionysus came into Greece from Thrace it is not unlikely that his earliest home was further east in the richer wine-lands of Asia Minor.[1]

The earliest known literary reference to the ecstasy comes to us from an Egyptian story of the eleventh century B.C. A certain prince, Wen-Amon by name, made an expedition to Byblos, in northern Syria, with the double purpose of making a commercial treaty and of introducing the worship of Amon, whose image was carried on one of

---

[1] For a fuller discussion of these points see the present writer's article, " Baal in Hellas " in the *Classical Quarterly* for October. 1917.

his ships. The governor of Byblos, Baal-Zeker, was unwilling to comply with either request, and daily sent down
to the harbour orders to Wen-Amon to return to Egypt.
After nineteen days the prince gave up hope, and one night
made all preparations for returning the next day. But in
the morning a message came saying that at a festival on
the previous evening a certain young noble of Byblos had
fallen into an ecstasy, and, speaking in the name of
the Baal of Byblos, had ordered that the new god,
Amon, and his servants should be received and duly
honoured.

This is amongst a Semitic people, as the name Baal-Zeker[1]
shows. But the ecstasy does not seem to have been a part
of the common heritage of the Semitic race. No trace of it
has yet been discovered in Babylonia, and in Arabia, where
it is to-day paralleled by the activities of some types of
Dervishes, it does not appear till well on in the history
of Islam. Even if it be held that the earlier visions of
Mohammed himself were something of this type, the very
fact that they did not win an immediate acceptance shews
that they were not recognised as being of divine origin.
The ecstasy is not characteristic of Israel in the nomadic
period. The only possible instance is that of the seventy
elders, a narrative in which later conditions may have been
read back into the past. Balaam is a genuine Ecstatic,
but he is not an Israelite, and probably comes from the
settled agricultural country of Moab. Any conjecture
must, in these circumstances, be extremely hazardous,
but it may be worth while commenting on the fact that the
original home of the ecstasy in religion seems clearly to
have included both Asia Minor and Palestine, and the only
known influence which covered both spheres and practically
nothing else is that of the Hittites. In our almost complete
ignorance of that mysterious race we may, perhaps, more

[1] i.e., " Baal remembers."

safely attribute the origin of ecstatic prophecy to them than to any others—at least till we learn the facts about them.

From what has been said it will be seen that in early times there was a very strong contrast between the Seer and the Nabi' in Israel. But there is a very important archæological note in I. Sam. ix. 9, which tells us that "the modern Nabi' was in ancient times called a Seer." This means that during the early monarchy the Seer properly so called disappeared, and that his characteristics and functions were assumed by the Nabi' or Ecstatic. That the "second sight" and "second hearing" became normal elements in the experience of the Nabi' is obvious, and it is possible that from the first he manifested these powers. A good instance may be seen in the case of Elisha's servant at Dothan.[1] Micaiah ben Yimlah, who withstood Ahab's prophets, is another case in point. It seems clear, then, that even if these powers did not belong to the earliest Nᵉbi'im, they were developed later, and the consciousness of the two worlds, the normal and the abnormal, became one of the most prominent features of the Ecstatic.

It is at first a little startling to realise that the Ecstatic was the direct ancestor of the Prophets whose words have been preserved for us in the Old Testament. It is true that the impression one receives from a study of the Nᵉbi'im is anything but favourable. It is also true that the great Canonical Prophets who followed them had a message to deliver such as the world had never heard before. In them first of all, men came to recognise that association of religion and morality, of righteousness and God, which is still the characteristic feature of Judaism and Christianity. To the superficial mind it will appear at first sight strange that a medium of this type should be

[1] II. Kings vi. 17.

employed for such a revelation. Even the thoughtful
student may feel something of a shock on realising that
men like Amos and Jeremiah were not readily distinguishable by their contemporaries from the Ecstatics whose
symptoms resembled those of the epileptic or even the
insane. Yet, pending further discussion as to whether the
canonical prophet really did look like the early Nabi',
two things may be said. The first is that the Divine revelation always proceeds from the known to the unknown.
The process is a gradual one, the slow building of tier upon
tier of truth, the disappearance from view of the lower
strata, and the steady increase in value and in permanence
of the higher courses, till the whole is seen to form part of
that perfect structure whose consummation lies far in the
future. The truth of God comes on the world not as a
lightning flash, but as the light of the dawn which shines
brighter and brighter till it reaches the full day. To the
Israel of 1000 B.C. a complete exposition of all that God
had to tell men would have been incomprehensible. In the
wilderness their ideas about God had been elementary,
and their religion had been contaminated in their settled
home by contact with the grossness of Canaanite practice.
In such circumstances much that was imperfect and
undesirable had to be left unchallenged in order that
the right stress might be laid on essentials, and that the
spiritual life of Israel might be led along paths which the
people as a whole might ultimately follow. In spite of all
crudity in the early Hebrew theology, there was something
in their knowledge and thought which could be modified,
even transformed. Whatever the faults of the early Nabi'
may have been, he was universally recognised as one in
whom God dwelt and through whom God spoke. It was
better that this imperfect medium should be employed for
the evolution of the world's faith, than that all accepted
notions as to the methods of God's dealings with man
should be violently overthrown. Israel knew that the

Prophet was a man of God, and the Prophet could thus
be used to show Israel what God was really like.

The second consideration is this : In spite of every
weakness and all ignorance, the Nabi' did stand for Yahweh.
He was, first and foremost, an enthusiast for his God. To
Him he owed his inspiration, and to Him he consecrated his
obedience. Not once but many times it fell to him to oppose
the gods who disputed Israel's allegiance with Yahweh.
The methods of these men were often iniquitous and cruel.
Their actions were marred by short-sightedness and
superstition. Their understanding of their God was
limited. Yet still they fought for Him, and, as best they
could, interpreted His will to His people. It was to
them more than to any others that Israel owed her learning
of her first lesson—" Thou shalt worship Yahweh thy God,
and Him only shalt thou serve." For it was only on this
basis that Israel could learn at all. It was in Yahweh that
she was ultimately to see the perfection of Godhead, but
this would never have appealed to her had she been free to
choose other gods and indulge in other rites. Before she
could begin to find out what her God was like, she must
devote herself utterly to Him. She had in the end to
offer to the world a picture of God immeasurably
superior to anything that had yet entered into the
mind of man, but till she had absorbed the lesson of personal
allegiance to Him, it was useless and perhaps impossible
to lift the first corner of the veil that hid the sublime
portrait from human gaze. So different was the Yahweh
whom the Jews worshipped in later times from the
conception elsewhere universal in popular thought, that
a single righteous God would never have been recognised
by the ancient Hebrew at all. It was only through
centuries of training that the revelation could come,
and the unwavering loyalty of Israel to Yahweh, the
uncompromising exclusion of all other rites and ideas, and
the absolute concentration upon the person of the national

God were necessary before the revelation could begin. The Nabi' was Yahweh's man in a special sense, and better than any other could insist that all Israelites must be Yahweh's men likewise.

IV

THE CANONICAL PROPHETS

A CERTAIN definite stage in the evolution of the Prophet,
as we understand the term to-day, was reached when one
of the individuals in the band separated himself and
delivered a message out of harmony with that of the rest.
The first person of whom this independence is recorded is
Micaiah.[1] The story goes that Ahab was contemplating
war against Damascus. Jehoshaphat, King of Judah, was
with him, and the two kings decided to make a common
expedition. It was necessary, first of all, to consult the
Prophets, who appeared before the kings in their normal
style and under the leadership of Zedekiah foretold the
victory. The King of Judah was not satisfied, and asked
if any other Prophet could be consulted. Ahab replied that
there was another, but that his utterances were invariably
unfavourable. Nevertheless Jehoshaphat insisted that he
should be summoned. Micaiah came, and his first reply
to Ahab's question was in full agreement with the opinion
of the other Prophets, but something in his tone or manner
made it clear that he was not speaking seriously, and Ahab
bade him tell the truth. Micaiah then uttered an oracle
in which he described how he had seen Israel scattered

---

[1] I. Kings xxii. 5-28.

P.P.I.A.S.—D

upon the mountains as sheep that had no shepherd. This could have only one meaning; Ahab was to be defeated and killed. His anger rose, and Micaiah proceeded to relate an ecstatic experience. He had seen the heavenly court, Yahweh surrounded by His attendant spirits. He had heard Yahweh ask for a volunteer to enter the mouth of the Prophets of Ahab and, by giving him a false promise of victory, to lure him to his doom. In the end it was Micaiah and not the other Prophets whose words came true. Part of the interest of the story lies in the belief, suggested elsewhere in the Old Testament, that Yahweh was capable of deceiving people to their ruin through the prophetic spirit. In fact the word for " entice " or " lure " seems to be used here and in other places in almost a technical sense.[1]

A century later the individual Prophet had become a familiar figure. It was no longer on the crowds of ecstatics that men relied for the divine message. It was rather the single independent speaker whose words they held to be due to the direct inspiration of Yahweh, but in all else it would seem that the canonical Prophet resembled the popular Nabi.' Doubt has been raised as to whether he was ecstatic at all, and not a few modern writers maintain that this element was entirely absent,[2] but this leaves three classes of facts without explanation.

The first of these facts is the language used of the Prophet. The word " Nabi' " applies to Amos, Hosea, Isaiah, and Jeremiah, just as much as to the Prophets of Baal, or to the companions of Zechariah. It may be remembered that these men whose words have come down to us were only a few amongst the many of their day. It is easy for us to see that these men were the true Prophets and

---

[1] *Cf.* Jer. xx. 7, Ez. xiv. 9.
[2] Especially Buttenwieser. Others are prepared to admit only an occasional or modified and more sober ecstasy.

that others were false. It was less easy for their contemporaries to make this distinction. In the light of our fuller knowledge it is possible for us to see the part that these men played in the development of the revelation of God. To those who were round about them it may have been difficult to decide which of two or more conflicting statements really had the divine authority. It was believed, as we have just seen, that Yahweh might deliberately mislead men through prophetic agency, and the Israelites may be pardoned if they preferred to accept the opinion of a majority of contemporary prophets, especially when that opinion was in full harmony with what they already believed about God's character and purpose. When we endeavour to explain the rejection of the prophetic message it is well for us to remember that there were few if any outward signs by which the true could be distinguished from the false. Other facts of this type seem to point in the same direction. The word "madman" used of the Nabi' who brought the final message to Jehu[1] is also applied by implication to Jeremiah[2]. The hostile priest of Bethel evidently regards Amos as being a Nabi' of the usual type, and employs the kindred word "Hinnabe'" of the Prophet's activities. This he could not have done if Amos had been merely an orator or preacher propounding moral truth.

Further, every indication of the actual experience of the Prophet points the same way. We may take the story of Isaiah's vision in the Temple. All the external things are real to him—the Temple walls and furniture, the altar and its fire—but there is that which is no part of the usual scene. The Prophet sees Yahweh Himself with his attendant winged serpents of blazing fire, he hears the voices alike of Yahweh and of the Seraph. The whole is marked by that second sight and that second hearing which was characteristic of the Prophets.

[1] II. Kings ix. 11.   [2] Jer. xxix. 26.

In the cases both of Amos and of Jeremiah we have the prophetic experience described. In the latter part of the Book of Amos there is a series of "visions" all of which are ecstatic in character. Thus Amos sees a plumb-line,[1] and the sight causes him to hear words spoken by Yahweh. In another instance he sees a locust,[2] in another a basket of fruit.[3] In two at least of these cases it seems clear that Amos is looking simply at the natural object. There is some conversation between himself and Yahweh, who asks what he is looking at, and develops the oracular message from the reply which the Prophet gives him. In one instance certainly that reply is based on a play on the word. What Amos sees is "Kais," "summer fruit," and from this comes the message of the "Kes," "the end" which is coming upon the Northern kingdom. It would seem that we have here a suggestion as to one of the ways in which the ecstasy took hold of the Prophet. He might be looking fixedly at a certain object, and its name, revolving in his mind, would bring home to him the substance of what he was to say. The dazed condition which often springs from such a fixed gaze would thus merge gradually into the actual experience of the ecstasy itself. Jeremiah, too, seems at times to have received his oracles in this way. The record goes that at the beginning of his ministry he received two "visions." In the one case he was looking at the almond branch—"shakéd"—and heard Yahweh telling him that he was awake—"shokéd"— over his word to perform it.[4] Again, he sees a pot in the open field boiling on the primitive earthern stove with all the smoke and steam blown southward by the north wind. This leads him to hear the voice of Yahweh telling him that from the north calamity will be blown.[5] On both occasions the message is introduced by a question from

---

[1] Am. vii. 7-9.   [2] Am. vii. 1-3.   [3] Am. viii. 1-2.   [4] Jer. i. 11, 12.
[5] Jer. i. 13 ff.

Yahweh as to what the Prophet is looking at. So, too, with the baskets of figs which he saw at a much later date, bringing him the message of contrast between the old nobility and the new.[1] But there are indications in the actual prophecies which suggest that the experience recorded was ecstatic. An example may be seen in Jeremiah[2] :—

I looked to the earth—and behold a chaos,
To the heavens—and their light was gone.
I looked to the hills—and lo, they quivered.
And all the mountains shook.
I looked—and behold, no man was there,
And all birds of the heaven were flown.
I looked to the cornland—and lo, a desert,
And all its cities were razed away.

The highest poetic imagination could hardly have achieved this. Jeremiah had seen the world dissolved into its primitive elements about him, and he felt the horror of heaving mountain and tossing hill, a burning lifeless world. It was as real to him as any other experience of his life—in other words, ecstatic.

It is thus probable that Isaiah, Amos, and Jeremiah were subject to the ecstasy, and the visions of Ezekiel and Zechariah may best be explained in the same way. It does not follow of necessity that all their utterances originated thus, yet it is at least possible.

Many of the prophetic oracles are introduced with the Hebrew phrase *Ko amar Yahweh*. This is normally rendered " Thus saith the Lord "—a translation of the verb for which there is very little grammatical justification. One of the visions of Amos already mentioned is introduced with the words " I saw " ; the rest by the phrase " Yahweh made me see." It appears in this case that the Prophet is

[1] Jer. xxiv.
[2] Jer. iv. 23-26, Skinner's translation (*Prophecy and Religion*, p. 37).

reporting an experience which is now past. There is no reason whatever for putting a different interpretation on the words " Thus said Yahweh." Where they are original in the introduction to an oracle (for no doubt they are often due to an editor or scribe), they also must be held to be a report of past experience. Just as in the one case an abnormal power of sight has been developed in the Prophet, so in the other case he has obtained abnormal powers of hearing. In other words, the commonest of all the phrases introducing the prophetic oracle suggests an ecstatic experience now past, which is being reported to the audience.[1]

The fact that the Prophet's message was thus given through an ecstatic experience does not deprive him of a personal share in its delivery. The experience of hypnotists tends to show that suggestion fails when the act suggested is out of harmony with the normal outlook and attitude of the subject. The hypnotic state is not the same as the ecstatic one, but there is sufficient resemblance to justify us in believing that this rule holds good in both cases. In the course of a long ministry such as that of Jeremiah, a man's views might undergo some change, especially if circumstances altered. We have no reason to doubt that a Prophet's ecstatic utterances were the expression of his own real opinions. The views he stated, the judgments he pronounced, the promises he made, may have been long in his mind ; but under normal conditions he did not feel free to utter them. They were to a large extent novel, and it was clear to him that they would be offensive. He needed for his own satisfaction some certainty that they were indeed the right thing, that there was nothing in them which was discordant with the will of Yahweh. The

---

[1] It seems not improbable that as time went on the wilder extravagances of the ecstasy disappeared, and that in the post-Exilic Prophets the second sight and second hearing alone remained.

occasion, too, for the delivery of the message must not be of his own seeking. The whole thing must be under the very seal of divine authority, and the only authority which he could fully accept was that which came to him through the ecstatic experience. Like others in his day, he believed that this was the true method of God's revelation to men, and to attempt to impress his views upon his contemporaries without such guarantee would have been to him an act of the highest presumption.

Finally, it may be noted that it was only through such means that men like Amos and Jeremiah could secure a hearing at all. Probably few would have taken any notice of them save those to whom their words appeared to be dangerous. To the ordinary Government official their message was nothing short of high treason. Indeed, it is quite clear that they must have been under some special protection, or their lives would not have been worth a moment's purchase. The ecstasy made it obvious that the speaker was justified in claiming the authority of Yahweh Himself, and therefore he must not be injured. It is a noteworthy fact that in the whole of the Old Testament there is only one instance of the execution of a Prophet.[2] That is the case of Uriah, put to death by Jehoiakim.[3] But that king always appears as the bold bad man, strong but unscrupulous, who feared not God neither regarded man. Amaziah dared not cut Amos' throat, and Zedekiah's courtiers had not the courage to kill Jeremiah outright. The worst they could do was to try to starve him,[4] and the

---

[1] A good instance is furnished by Jeremiah's escape from the Priests and the Nᵉbi'im, recorded in Jer. xxvi. *Cf.* especially v. 16.

[2] The slaughter of the Prophets of Baal by Elijah (I. Kings xviii. 40) is in a different category, for it was intended as a challenge to, and a renunciation of, the god whom they claimed to represent. A man would do to a foreign or hostile god what he would not do to his own national deity.

[3] Jer. xxvi. 23.

[4] Jer. xxxviii. 1-13.

East sees murder only in the actual striking of the fatal blow. It is clear that the persons of these two men were recognised as sacrosanct. The spirit of Yahweh possessed them, and whether their words were true or false, they themselves were inviolable. The ecstasy, both to the Prophet and to his hearers, was a guarantee of Yahweh's presence and message.

In the case of the Prophets whose words have come down to us in the Old Testament, that message was of unique value. Its importance does not lie in the fact that they were able to foretell the future, for prediction, though one of their functions, was accidental and not fundamental. There are eternal " laws " in the moral, social, and spiritual realms, just as much as in the physical. The discovery of these latter, their statement and formulation, the uses to which they may be put and the perils which threaten those who disregard them—these are the tasks which are laid upon the physical scientist. The Prophet was in some sort a spiritual scientist. It was his to study the mind of God in His dealings with men. He had to discover the Divine attitude towards human relationships, an attitude expressed not in an arbitrary system of rewards and punishments, but in a reasonable chain of cause and effect. To him was granted the insight, born of direct communication with God, to see with startling clarity that a given type of conduct, still more a given attitude of soul, carried within itself the seeds of prosperity or disaster. The punishment of sin—and their lot was cast in ages when the punishment of sin was far more obvious than the reward of righteousness—is not the petulant vindictiveness of irritated Omnipotence, it is the reverse side of the medal whereof the sinner at the moment of his act sees only the obverse. Crime and penalty are not two distinct and separable facts—they are one and the same, seen merely from different angles and on different sides.

It was from this knowledge of law that the Prophet was able to predict the future. An astronomer who is familiar with the " law " of gravitation can foretell for thousands of years the exact movements of the heavenly bodies. A chemist will state with unfailing accuracy the reaction which will take place when certain substances are combined. In just the same way the Prophet, an earnest and faithful student of God's laws in religion and ethics, will state with equal accuracy the issue of a social condition or of a spiritual attitude. One must not, however, look too closely for details, nor are such commonly elaborated, but the main principles are always reliable. At the same time, prophetic prediction is necessarily conditional. If men change their point of view or modify their line of conduct, it follows that a new factor has been introduced into the combination, and that the result will inevitably be affected accordingly. This hypothetical element in prophecy is not always expressed, but it is always there, and allowance must be made for it in attempting to estimate the predictive character of a Prophet's work.

Further, behind all " law," whether physical or spiritual, stands the being and character of God. The Prophet was no metaphysician. It may be true that God is more than a person, and that the philosopher may be right in insisting that personality is only one of His attributes. Nevertheless it is that aspect of His nature with which man always has to deal in practical religion. The Prophets saw God as a Person, and ever in that light interpreted His attitude to man. Hence their task included—and this was perhaps its supreme function—the exposition of the *character* of God. His righteousness, His holiness, and His love were the high themes of their investigation. Above all they had to insist on the practical application of these qualities to the life of the nation, and, later, to that of the individual.

The Prophet thus discovered and proclaimed eternal verities. Yet the garb in which he clothed them was essentially the fashion of his own age. The language, metaphor, style, and still more the " thought-shape " were such as were current amongst his compatriots and contemporaries. Further, his message was always addressed to a particular occasion and adapted to particular circumstances. This, if one may so speak in all reverence, is God's true method of revelation. The appreciation of Divine truth must be inductive, proceeding from given instances to generalised statements. An abstract disquisition on ethical or theological doctrine would have been meaningless and ineffectual in its own day, and would inevitably have perished with its purpose unfulfilled. Whilst in all cases a practical and pointed application of truth to an immediate condition is the best means of bringing that truth home to men, it was perhaps more necessary amongst Semitic races than anywhere else. A comparison of the Old Testament with the Koran, that other great monument of Semitic religious literature, shows how small a part the reflective and speculative types of thought had in their production. All is direct, concrete, practical, aimed at meeting the need of the hour, yet seeking to apply, perhaps only half consciously, principles as enduring as personality itself.

The task, then, of the modern interpreter of the Prophets, is a double one. He is dealing with truth, eternal indeed, yet held in the solution of a certain age and of a certain people. He who would apply the message thus presented to the conditions of his own day must first crystallise out the truth itself. He must distinguish between the substance and the solvent. The generalisation, the universal, is rarely upon the surface of the prophetic utterance ; it must be discovered and clearly stated if its final purpose is to be attained.

This done, a new solvent is to hand in modern conditions, modern speech, and the modern outlook. The meaning of

God for human life needs to be stated in these terms also if its permanent efficiency is to be secured. There are times indeed when this double process is startlingly easy. Not once but often in human history have similar conditions appeared. With comparatively slight alterations of outward form it is possible to see reproduced in the modern world the position of ancient Samaria, Jerusalem, or Babylon. In reading such books as Amos or Hosea we are repeatedly struck by their extraordinary suitability for present conditions. God is still God, man is still man, and the essential message of every true Prophet is as valid for our own day as it was for his.

V

THE STRUCTURE OF THE PROPHETIC BOOKS.

WE can now call before our minds a picture of the Prophet's activity in public. He might be mingling with the crowd, sometimes on ordinary days, sometimes on special occasions. Suddenly something would happen to him. His eye would become fixed, strange convulsions would seize upon his limbs, the form of his speech would change. Men would recognise that the Spirit had fallen upon him. The fit would pass, and he would tell to those who stood around the things which he had seen and heard. There might have been symbolic action, and this he would explain with a clear memory of all that had befallen him, and of all that he had done under the stress of the ecstasy. Such manifestations were common, and there were many who were subject to them. The message of most of these was for their own time, and for their own circumstances, but a few at different times and at different places were recognised as uttering truths of eternal value. Words such as these could not be allowed to perish, they would be remembered and repeated, and at last be committed to writing. They would thus pass from hand to hand, copies would be made, and there must have been many of these written oracles in the possession of the people of Israel. It does not seem that the earliest of the Prophets—Amos, Hosea, and Micah—themselves attempted to build their utterances into books. Isaiah certainly felt the desirability of preserving his message for generations to come, and entrusted some of his oracles to writing.[1] He also gathered around him a small company who retained his words in their memory and handed them on to their successors.[2] At the same time it is not impossible that Amos, Hosea, and Micah themselves collected and edited these scattered utterances, and so produced the substance of the books we now possess ; but this is not certain, and in view of the form the books themselves take, it is unlikely.

The first of the Prophets who is known to have collected or recalled his own words to any large extent was Jeremiah. The story is familiar. For some reason or other he was prevented from public appearance, but the disaster of Carchemish, and the final overthrow of the Egyptian power, impelled him to repeat to his people what Yahweh had revealed to him in earlier days. He therefore summoned Baruch, a professional writer, and dictated to him the messages of the past twenty years. These were then read in public assembly, and as a result the volume was destroyed by Jehoiakim. A second volume, containing the same material, was prepared in a similar way, and until Jerusalem fell, the Prophet kept this by him, having additions made where he felt it to be necessary.[3]

It is quite clear that this volume was far from including all that is now contained in the book of Jeremiah, and it is only when we reach Ezekiel that we find the Prophet depending more on the written than on the spoken word. In this respect he seems to have been followed by Haggai and Zechariah, but by practically no other Israelite Prophet. Most of them seem to have been content to leave the preservation of their message to the memories of those who heard them, and there is nothing which definitely proves that any of them was interested in the literary conservation of his work.

[1] Is. xxx. 8.   [2] Is. viii. 16.   [3] Jer. xxxvi.

We still have to ask ourselves what was the process which ultimately produced the prophetic books. At the first stage we have already glanced—the committal of the separate utterances to writing.

To each of these we may give the name " oracle," understanding by that term the message given at any one time and through any one ecstatic experience. There is no reason to believe that this experience was commonly of long duration, though Ezekiel sometimes remained in a state of trance for days together. In any case it seems clear that the oracle itself—that is, the words in which the message was enshrined, was almost always short, and consisted of a few sentences which would drive home the point in unforgettable fashion. Further, it would seem that the oracle was always cast in poetic form, that it was, in fact, a short poem of the characteristic Hebrew type. It is this fact which enables us to ascertain something of the structure of the prophetic books. The Hebrew was not reflective, and the ecstatic experience tended to produce emotional expression rather than logical consistency. The result is that one does not look in the individual oracle for more than one dominant idea. It is not a reasoned process of thought that is attempted. The prophetic oracle is rather an effort to bring home a single truth in arresting language and striking phrases.

If, then, in reading one of the prophetic books, we find ourselves suddenly transferred from one sphere of thought to another, sometimes even from one metaphor to another, we may guess that we have a new oracle. This in itself is a valuable help in trying to determine the structure of the book, but there are other indications. One of these is to be found in the presence of introductory or concluding phrases. Not infrequently " Thus saith the Lord " appears at the beginning of the oracle, and the words " Saith the Lord " are at the end. These alone are usually decisive where they are original, though in many cases they are absent, and in many are due to the mistakes of copyists, or have been inserted by editors.

The third indication may be sought in the poetic rhythm. There is no reason to believe that we have any elaborate versification in the prophetic books. The shortness of the oracles would in itself make this impossible, but there is equally little reason to deny the existence of poetic form in the speech of the Prophets. It is also fairly clear that, within the limits of an individual poem, the dominant "metre" remained unchanged. It is sometimes difficult, for various reasons, to be certain of the original "metre" of a short poem, but where this can be definitely ascertained, and we find ourselves passing from one rhythm into another, we may be practically certain that we have reached the end of one oracle and have started a fresh one.

We have no means of deciding when or where these oracles were first written down. They may have been retained in the memories of the hearers for weeks, months, or even years. The art of writing, whilst familiar, was not widely spread, and, as at the present day in the East, was largely confined to a professional class. But the facts make it perfectly clear that the first step was the writing down of the separate oracles. Who wrote them is another question which, in the majority of cases, it is impossible to answer. At the same time, there is no reason to doubt that most of the prophetic oracles were definitely associated with some Prophet or other when they were first committed to writing.

Others, it is true, carried no special name, and it was left to later ages to connect them with one or other of the well-known Prophets. Whether named or not, it is clear that these oracles, separate and independent as they were, continued to be copied and re-copied by people who were interested in their contents.

It is only natural that men so interested should desire to possess and to keep together more than one oracle

uttered by their favourite Prophet. There thus grew up
a number of small collections of oracular matter. The
grounds on which this matter was selected and put together
varied considerably. Sometimes the basis of the collection
would be merely the belief that all were to be assigned
to the same Prophet, in other cases identity or similarity
of subject would be responsible for their association.
Oracles directed against foreign nations seem to have
had a peculiar fascination for these early compilers. Thus
in the books of Isaiah, Jeremiah, Ezekiel and Amos, we
have collections of such oracles included in the body of
the book. Even where there was no doubt as to the origin,
a Prophet's utterances on the neighbours of Israel were
isolated from the rest of his work and kept together. This
appears to have been done by Ezekiel himself as far as his
own prophecies were concerned, for all the evidence suggests
that he was his own compiler. In one instance, that of
Obadiah, the book consists entirely of a collection of
prophecies directed against Edom, and the fact that some
of these occur in a similar collection in the book of Jeremiah
suggests that they were for the most part unnamed. The
word Obadiah means simply "Servant of Yahweh," and it
is quite possible that the name was attached to the collected
book because it was one that would suit any Prophet.
In the actual arrangement of the oracles within a collection
the compilers often displayed ingenuity and skill, and
sometimes deep spiritual insight. They were fond, for
instance, of putting side by side oracles which had only
a superficial resemblance, due to the presence of the same
or similar phrases in both. Thus in Is. i. the oracle which
ends with verse 9 introduces a reference to Sodom and
Gomorrah. The same two names appear at the beginning
of the next oracle, though the subject is entirely different,
and the oracles are absolutely independent of one another.
This recurrence of the names is clearly the reason why
the compiler places the two together. It is also possible

that from time to time oracles which were originally separate were woven together into an artistic whole. A formula or refrain might be introduced, and the complete product would then present the appearance of a strophic poem Some compilers show a real historic sense in the arrangement of their material. In Is. xl.—xlviii., for instance, there is every appearance of chronological order, and it is possible to follow with some accuracy the events which led to the fall of Babylon. It is in such cases as this that we most readily suspect the Prophet of having been his own compiler.

We have thus reached the second stage in the evolution of the prophetic books, a condition in which we have no longer a floating mass of scattered oracles, but little booklets of oracular matter, most of which carry the name of some well-known Prophet. At the same time some oracles continue to maintain a separate existence, and if they had no name were liable to be included in more than one collection. This will explain the presence of the same oracles against Edom in the Books of Obadiah and Jeremiah, the same oracles against Moab in the Books of Isaiah and Jeremiah, and the same oracle in Is. ii. 2-4 and Mi. iv. 1-4. Clearly these were anonymous " floating " oracles which different collectors attributed to different Prophets. Another curious instance is furnished by the Book of Jeremiah, where an oracle occurs applied to Judah in vi. 22-26 and to Babylon in l. 41-43, though in the second case in a mutilated form. This is, further, an instance of the way in which a floating oracle might readily be included in a collection dealing with a foreign nation.

It has already been remarked that in most cases there is no strong reason to believe that the Prophet was responsible for the writing down or collection of the great mass of the oracles attributed to him. Isaiah wrote something for future generations to read, though it does not seem that the amount was large, being apparently confined to an utterance against Samaria.[1] Jeremiah made a real collection of his earlier messages, though it is by no means clear whether that collection is included in our present book, or the extent which it covers if it is included.[2] It seems that Ezekiel, Haggai, and Zechariah, really did write practically the whole of what has come down to us under their respective names, and prepared their books in much the form they have now. There are a few well marked characteristics which distinguish the prophetic matter so transmitted.

The divisions in these collections are frequently dated in some detail. This may, of course, have been the work of an editor, but it is significant that such dating does not normally occur in other collections. It frequently happens that narratives *about* the Prophet are thus dated, but the regular poetic collection of oracles or the individual oracle itself practically never. The nearest approach to dating occurs when the occasion is indicated. The three books mentioned are, as a matter of fact, the only ones in which dates occur, except in historical sections. There are, of course, cases in which matter written down or dictated by a Prophet has no date. This seems certain in the case of Jeremiah and Isaiah, and is probably true of a good deal of Ezekiel, possibly also of Zechariah. But as a general rule it may be held that the dated sections of prophecy were written and compiled either by the Prophet himself or under his immediate superintendence.

In the second place, such sections are nearly always in narrative form, and are given in the first person. It is this latter feature which distinguishes them from the bio-graphical passages which are occasionally met with, especially in the Book of Jeremiah. They sometimes give a note as to the circumstances in which the message was delivered, more often not. But they always describe in greater or less detail the actual experience of the Prophet.

[1] *Cf.* Is. xxx. 8.   [2] *Cf.* Jer. xxxvi.   [3] This refers only to chs. i.-viii.

Sometimes this is an account of what he saw, more often merely of what he heard for transmission to his audience. One description of such personal experience occurs in Isaiah (ch. vi.), one in Hosea (ch. iii.), several in Amos (in chs. vii.-ix.). There are a number in Jeremiah, they are frequent in Ezekiel, and the Books of Haggai and Zechariah i.-viii. are in this form throughout.

These narratives, too, are much more literary in form than the separate oracle. That is to say, they are intended to be read rather than heard. Usually they are in prose, but there are cases, especially in Ezekiel, where they form a somewhat long and artistic poem. Apart from those sections which describe the prophet's call, they contain oracular matter, but this has generally been reduced to prose in transcription. The prose style is that which is natural to the age and period of the Prophet, and might be used in case of doubt as some indication of his date. Is. vi. is in prose. So are many of the autobiographical passages in Jeremiah, Amos, and Hosea. Ezekiel contains a few poems, but Haggai and Zechariah are prose throughout.

But it would seem that there was other literary material which was concerned with the Prophets. Reference has already been made to narratives about them. Numbers of these, most of them dealing with the earlier N^ebi'im, were employed by the compilers of Kings. Others were not so used, but have remained independent. Thus we have much in I. Kings about Elijah, and in II. Kings about Elisha and Isaiah, the chapters which refer to the latter appearing again in the Book of Isaiah with some modifications. Other biographical narratives do not appear outside the prophetic book itself. Such are the story of Hosea's marriage in ch. i., the account of the clash between Amos and Amaziah in Am. vii., and a considerable portion of the Book of Jeremiah, especially in chs. xxvi. and onwards.

This leads us on to the next step. It is quite clear that the separate booklets whose compilation marks the second stage were gradually combined into larger volumes. Sometimes narrative matter was introduced, and sometimes the booklets were placed side by side, each with its original title and heading. Sometimes the narrative matter would be broken up, and the compiler would employ it by taking its sections and using them as introductions to the booklets which he was combining. In the Book of Isaiah, for instance, the greater part of the historical matter is collected into chs. xxxvi.-xxxix. In the Book of Jeremiah, on the other hand, the three types of material are combined in accordance with a fairly consistent plan. Other matter might be inserted at the beginning or close of each booklet, though this is seldom more than a mere note.

One other point remains to be mentioned. At some time after the Exile, but before the beginning of the second century, the prophetic books themselves were collected and arranged in four volumes of roughly equal size. This made it necessary to include in some of the volumes the work of more than one Prophet. Thus one is still known by the name of " The Book of the Twelve." But there were also included collections to which no name was attached at all. In the process of repeated copying, the divisions between these and the preceding collections became obscured, and so it has happened that in several instances we have two or three collections grouped under the name of a single Prophet. In the case of Isaiah, for instance, we have two considerable collections which may have been united by a compiler before they were placed after the Book in which they are now commonly included, but were originally quite independent both of it and of each other. The same accident seems to have been responsible for the present form of the Book of Micah and of the Book of Zechariah. In the case of Obadiah and Malachi the independence of an anonymous[1]

---

[1] It should be remarked that many scholars still believe that these books were the works of the men whose names appear at their head.

collection was secured by the appearance of a separate name at its head.

We have succeeded in tracing the growth of our prophetic books out of the primitive material of which they were composed. It will readily be seen that the process of growth varied in different cases. In some the construction of the book may have been undertaken by the Prophet himself, in others by his immediate hearers. In yet other cases centuries elapsed between the time when the burning words first fell from his lips and the age when the book was completed. So in the course of generations a small nucleus of oracular matter would gather round it numerous additions and accretions whose source it is no longer possible to trace. Yet we cannot regret this process. We have no reason or right to limit the Divine inspiration to that small number of men whose names appear at the head of our prophetic books, and it may well be that some of the most cherished messages that God has ever bestowed on man have reached us through nameless Prophets whose life is utterly unknown to us, and whose work has come down to us only in brief snatches and minute sections.[1]

---

[1] Some of the noblest of prophetic utterances are probably anonymous, *e.g.* Is. ii. 2-4 (=Mi. iv. 1-4). and Mi. vi. 8.

VI

AMOS.

THERE is a certain sense in which every reformer is the
product and representative of his age. The man who brings
home a fresh revelation of truth must of necessity find a
basis to which he can appeal in the thought of his contemporaries, or his work is futile. Whilst we associate
the Reformation with such names as Luther, Calvin and
Zwingli, there had been within the Church for centuries
the spirit of reform, often repressed, yet never entirely
absent, and the new movement was made possible largely
by the surging impulse of intellectual vitality for which the
Renaissance was responsible. So without in the least degree
detracting from the value of the work of Amos and his
successors, we may reasonably conjecture that the way
had in some measure been prepared for them, and that
there was in some Israelite quarters an attitude which
made for an ultimate acceptance of their teaching.

We have already seen[1] that the contamination of Hebrew
religion by that of Canaan was by no means uniform.
Whilst in the richer and more "civilised" parts of the
country the religion of Israel hardly differed from that
of her predecessors except in the name she gave to her

---

[1] See ch. II.

national God, there were also many living on the borders, especially in the south and east, who retained to a large extent the habits and the outlook of the desert. To them the ethic of Samaria was abhorrent, for they clung to the simpler and purer standards of the pastoral life. Their best known representative in early days was Elijah. Though less conspicuously a typical Nabi' than Elisha, he was more truly the forerunner of the canonical Prophets. It will be remembered that the protest he made against the court was a double one. He opposed and condemned the worship of the Tyrian Baal, but he spoke with equal vehemence on the subject of Jezebel's treatment of Naboth. Thus, even in the middle of the ninth century, one of the most powerful and striking personalities in Hebrew history combined the interests of Yahweh and righteousness. It is true that he stood to some extent alone —or had reason to believe himself to stand alone—and to all outward appearance his message and work left no permanent mark on the life of the Northern kingdom ; but it may well be that his efforts so affected the thinking of his people that when men like Amos appeared it was recognised that their message was a valid one and should be preserved, even though the mass of his contemporaries were not prepared to accept it. He had his place in the stream of revelation.

Amos, too, was a man of somewhat the same type. His home was in Tekoa, amongst the wilder hills of the far south. His main occupation was that of a shepherd,[1] though he seems to have added to this livelihood the culture of a kind of coarse fig characteristic of the desert border. In all his life he had never been exposed to the dangers accompanying a fair amount of leisure, a luxurious standard of comfort and the possibility of great wealth. At the same time it is probable that the community in

[1] Am. vii. 15.

which he was brought up was free from the grosser elements
in the religious life of the landowner and the city dweller.

We can, then, picture to ourselves the startling contrast
presented to his eyes when first he came into contact with
Samaritan luxury. He brought with him a freedom of
spirit and an independence of outlook which saved him
from the numbing influence of familiarity. It is not easy
for men to stand aside and form a fair judgment on the
community in which they have been brought up, and even
when they realise that things are wrong, they are apt to
be oppressed by the knowledge that they cannot escape
from personal complicity. This is emphatically not true of
Amos. He has been accustomed all his life to the wide
spaces of the south, to the bare hills on whose slopes
travellers are so rare that the presence of two together
can be no accident, but must have been pre-arranged.[1]
To him the sky has been a dome of expansive grandeur in
whose blue depths he has watched the slow wheeling
flight of the vulture, till some dying creature, it may be
miles away, has attracted its glance, and it has grown in
one rapid swoop from a circling speck to the largest of
winged things.[2] He has heard and understood the hollow
roar of the lion as he leaped on his prey in the jungles of
the marshy bottoms.[3] He has met the bear, the most
dreaded of four-footed beasts, and has seen snakes coiled
in the holes of crumbling walls.[4] The things that are most
familiar to him are those of the outdoor world, and from
his varied experience of nature he comes to the complicated
and artificial life of the city with an amazing clarity of
vision which reaches far below the surface and penetrates
the most familiar disguise. It was, perhaps, only such a
man as this who could see the rotting civilisation of Samaria
as it really was, and could give to her habits and customs
the right and proper names. Long familiarity with

---

[1] *Cf.* iii. 3   [2] *Cf.* iii. 5.   [3] *Cf.* iii. 4-8.   [4] *Cf.* v. 19.

conditions may well have blinded the citizen and the farmer to the contradiction between religion and morality. But this man, from his simpler life and more primitive worship, did not hesitate, with unparalleled audacity, to correlate religion and ethics, and to propound the unique, amazing, and epoch-making doctrine that :

> " Nothing can be good in Him,
> Which evil is in me."

For there can be no doubt as to the rottenness of that society in which Amos found himself at Bethel. Years of cruel border warfare had tended to depress and impoverish the tillers of the soil. The comparative freedom which had been enjoyed since the decline of the power of Damascus had brought but little relief to the " lower " classes. For there had flowed into the great cities a wealth which was no longer the product of the exertions of the citizens themselves, applied directly to the natural resources of their own country. It would seem that the markets of almost the whole known world were now open to Israel, and from her central position she could levy a formal or informal toll on all the merchandise that passed from Asia to Africa and *vice versa*. It is clear that there was fully developed, at the same time, the dangerous habit of making money for its own sake. With the rise of money-lending as a profession, it was inevitable that avarice would work its effects on the body politic. Agricultural operations from time to time need assistance of this kind, and it is at least likely that there had always been some sort of restriction on the extent to which an owner of money might profit by his neighbour's misfortunes. Such limits were, however, no longer observed. The small farmer who failed to redeem his mortgage lost his land, and was probably allowed to cultivate it on behalf of the new owner, paying a fairly large portion of the produce as rent. Land-grabbing of this kind was one of the crimes most strenuously denounced by men like Amos and Isaiah, and the former

has bitter complaints of the people who took the best part
of the crops as rent from their tenants.[1] As not infrequently
happens in the East, the wealthy had the legal machinery
on their side. It would seem that such a case as that
involved in foreclosing on a mortgage had to come before
a court of some kind. No form of social wrong is more
common in the oriental lands than the corruption of justice.
The venality of those on whom rested the duty of giving
decisions is one of the most prominent features of the
condemnations which Amos uttered.[2] Even the smallest
bribe—a pair of shoes might do—would be enough to secure
a verdict, and hand over to the new master not only the
land, but in some cases the farmer himself and his family.
It is possible that men sometimes even went so far as to
make a claim of this kind when there was no loan at all, and
the case had not the slightest justificationi n fact or in law.

Hand in hand with the oppression of the poor went the
shallow luxury of the rich. One is inevitably reminded
of the pictures of the French aristocratic life before the
Revolution. Greedy, selfish, and shameless women,[3]
tasteless domestic ostentation,[4] Jingoism and national
conceit[5]—these were the most striking elements in the
ordinary life of the townsfolk as Amos saw them. Further,
the claims of religion exercised no restraining influence.
On the contrary, the demands of worship and ritual were
not seldom invoked to shelter some unusually iniquitous
conduct. The common law of Israel provided that if a
man's outer garment, the simple robe that serves as a
cloak, a cushion, a mattress, or a coverlet to the oriental
peasant, were accepted as security against a debt, it must
be restored to its owner for the night, lest he suffer too
greatly from the cold. But there was an exception to the
law, and if the lender of the money could make the excuse

---

[1] *Cf.* v. 11.   [2] *Cf.* ii. 6, v. 7, 12, 15 ; vi. 12.   [3] *Cf.* iv. 1-3.
[4] *Cf.* vi. 1-7.   [5] *Cf.* vi. 13.

that he needed the article for some sacred ceremony, such as "incubation," he felt no obligation to return it. Violence and oppression were held to be justified if they were the means whereby wine could be secured for the sacramental meals in the Temples.[1] Fornication—and that in some of its most loathsome forms—was practised in connection with the worship of Yahweh Himself, and He was made the scapegoat for any moral wrong that might be involved. If anybody was ethically guilty in the matter, it was not the man who did the act, but the God who demanded it— or was supposed to demand it.[2] Even where the cultus was not stained with grosser forms of wickedness, it was an external thing, a matter at best of elaborate ritual,[3] the rigid observance of outward forms and feasts, with no spiritual or even mental consecration to correspond.[4] Of the conception of religion as a personal and spiritual relationship with a morally holy God, Amos found no trace in the worship of the sanctuaries of his day.

It seemed, indeed, as if nothing could touch the conscience of Israel. Disasters that befell other peoples were attributed to the whimsical and unreasoning patriotism of her God. No honest critic could secure a hearing.[5] Blow after blow had fallen upon Israel herself, yet she utterly failed to connect her misfortunes with Yahweh's passion for righteousness. Famine, drought, blight, epidemic disease, earthquake, eclipse—if these things were recognised as the work of Yahweh, they were supposed to be a demand only for a more strenuous religiosity. Vice and crime on the one hand and sin on the other stood over against one another; it never seems to have occurred to the average man in Samaria that these things were really one, and that Yahweh was concerned with them all.[6] If attention were called to the facts and to their ethical implications, the bold speaker

---

[1] *Cf.* ii. 8.   [2] *Cf.* ii. 7.   [3] *Cf.* v. 21-27.   [4] *Cf.* iv. 4, 5.
[5] *Cf.* v. 10.   [6] *Cf.* iv. 6-11.

was promptly charged with treasonable aims. An honest prophet was beyond the experience of the men of Jeroboam II. For nearly a century, when the inspired man had interfered in public matters, his motives had been political. The revolution which had placed on the throne that very dynasty to which Jeroboam belonged had been engineered by the " N^ebi'im," and Amos himself was only protected by the superstition which held his ecstasy sacrosanct.[1] The spiritual starvation with which the southern prophet threatened the people had already been their lot for three generations past.[2] The faculty for God had been suppressed to the point of atrophy.

It is part of the greatness of Amos that he saw and understood all this ; part of his greatness, but not the whole of it. If we would realise his full importance, it is necessary to see him not only in contrast with those whom he condemned, but equally in contrast with others who stood as he did for the simpler and purer outlook of more primitive Israel. For in his instinct for a better life and in his sense of iniquity Amos did not stand alone. The syncretism which had connected all the sins of Israel with religion had naturally affected only those who were concerned with the operations of agriculture, and lived in the more fertile lands. In the wilder hills, where Israel had first established herself, in the great desert spaces which nurtured that hardier type to which Amos himself belonged, there were still those who clung to the earlier and more truly Mosaic form of religion. This double tradition of Israelite faith is not always obvious. but there are indications which point surely to its existence, It was not an accident that Elijah himself, the forerunner of the great ethical prophets, came also out of the wild.[3] And even in the heart of the land there were tribes and groups who stood for the pure cult of nomadic times. Such

---

[1] *Cf.* vii. 10-17.   [2] *Cf.* viii. 11, 12.

[3] It will be remembered that Zarathustra also belonged to a simple shepherd people still at the pastoral stage of social organisation

were the Rechabites and the Nazirites, who, in spite of
every temptation and possibly of persecution,[1] still clung to
their testimony.

The Nazirite and the Rechabite, however, had one remedy
for the diseases of Israel, Amos had another. To them the
evil was civilisation, and was to be cured only by the most
drastic social surgery. All this elaboration and complica-
tion of life was something strange, foreign to the genius
of Israel, and therefore to be avoided by all true worshippers
of Yahweh. The difficulties could be met only by abolishing
the whole scheme of life as practised by Samaria, and
reverting to the habits of the desert even in a rich and fertile
land. The newer manners and customs had proved a source
of temptation ; righteousness could be attained only by
the disappearance of that temptation. Such a position
was only natural to an honest, enthusiastic, but short-
sighted man. It is inevitable that fresh conditions of life
should bring with them fresh possibilities of evil. It is
almost equally inevitable that men who stand for righteousness should see in the new conditions the *fons et origo mali,*
the spring of all the rottenness and corruption of their
time. It is impossible not to sympathise with such a position.
We may be inclined to speak of it as narrow-minded, but it
does make for character, and it does help to keep alive the
sense for goodness in conduct. No doubt it tends to develop
into casuistry and superficial hypocrisy—perhaps worse
dangers than the more obvious forms of wrongdoing—but
it does testify to the existence of a moral ideal. Yet its
methods are inevitably conservative, and even retrograde.
It ignores the truth that wherever there is real life there
must also be growth. There is an evolutionary element
in social life as well as in physical life, and in the long run
the one is no more to be checked without peril than the
other. Humanity moves forward and not backwards ;

[1] *Cf.* ii. 11, 12.

a social order may come to a catastrophic end, but it cannot retrace its steps. It is at best only a piece of machinery, and it is entirely dependent for its efficiency on the motive force which lies behind it. Given that, the machinery suitable to it will in time be evolved, but a permanent lack of harmony between the machinery and the motive force can only be disastrous. Though men do not commonly realise it, each new stage in human society is an experiment, an adventure, and safety can only be secured, not by returning to the paths already forsaken, but by adapting a growing spiritual life to the needs and conditions of the fresh discovery. Such a state of affairs as that which confronted Amos is the result of a growth in the externals of social and political life with which the soul of the community has failed to keep pace. The true cure is not to attempt a reversion to the old ways, as the Nazirite and the Rechabite would have done, but to apply to the new ways the spiritual and moral principles which had made for the highest success in the old.

It is in his appreciation of this truth that the real greatness of Amos lies. He did not denounce the system as a system ; he said, in effect, that it must be worked on the principles which Israel had already learnt from Yahweh in the desert. The supreme failure was not that Israel had learnt to plough and Samaria to trade, but that neither had seen that Yahweh was concerned in both activities. In the desert the highest religious and ethical conduct might consist in keeping the Passover, in not seething a kid in its mother's milk, in observing the elementary laws of property and maintaining the obligations of blood-relationship. These things were not wrong in themselves, but, unless supplemented by something more, they were quite inadequate to the conditions of Palestinian life They were the expression of principles in a form which was natural and suitable to the nomadic life ; these same principles must be crystallised out of that life, and re-dissolved in conduct

which would make it possible to apply them to the market
and to the farm.

First and foremost amongst the doctrines of Amos is
the truth of the universality of Yahweh. This is not yet
necessarily monotheism, though it must in time develop
into monotheism. But men are very slow to realise the
logical results of their own views, and it may well be that
the supremacy of the God of Israel had to wait for many
years before it could grow into the more finished theological
and philosophical theory of a single God. But Amos
certainly did realise and proclaim the truth that Yahweh
is supreme. Other gods are mentioned,[1] but mentioned
with a certain contempt. Real or not, they were inferior,
and Israel should have nothing whatever to do with them.
On the other hand, Yahweh had made the whole world.
He had set the heavenly bodies in their orbits, and still
controlled their movements.[2] The expanse of earth and
the dome of heaven were alike the products of His activity.[3]
All human history, too, was the outcome of His will. He
was interested in Israel, it is true,[4] but He was also
concerned with other peoples and nations. Even the great
racial migrations were undertaken at His behest, though
those most concerned in them were ignorant of the fact.[5]
Still more did He appear as the vindicator of universal
moral laws. He would punish the neighbouring tribes,
not merely as the patriot-god, for wrongs done to Israel,
but for crimes which violated the natural laws of common
humanity, whoever the victims might be.[6] Israelite God
as He was, He was still more the God of righteousness.
His special relationship to His own people meant, not
privilege to do wrong, but responsibility to do right.[7] It
was Israel that must adapt herself to this conception of
a universal moral law, not Yahweh, who must consider

---

[1] *Cf.* v. 26.   [2] *Cf.* v. 8.   [3] *Cf.* iv. 13.   [4] *Cf.* iii. 2.   [5] *Cf.* ix. 7.
[6] *Cf.* the oracles against foreign nations in i. and ii.   [7] *Cf.* iii. 2.

primarily the material advantage of Israel. If she failed here—and this is the real essence of the teaching of Amos—she lost her only *raison d'être*, and, so far from protecting her, Yahweh would Himself ordain her ruin. Every nation, every sphere of life, was subject to these supreme laws, and the real function of Israel amongst the civilised peoples of the world was to work them out in her common life. Sacrifice, as compared with this, was insignificant, and without this a mockery. Religion consists in getting into touch with God, and it is impossible to get into touch with a God who is supreme righteousness without at least making righteousness an essential element in the religious ideal.

It is this contrast between the great purpose of Yahweh and the failure of Israel to appreciate it that is responsible for the tone of most of Amos' utterances. The people must either bring the ultimate principles for which Yahweh stood into their daily life, or they must perish. The prophet's premises admitted of no alternative conclusion. Of the reform which was required there was little or no sign. Therefore every means at Yahweh's disposal would be employed to bring about the ruin of the nation. Natural calamities—drought,[1] pestilence,[2] earthquake,[3]—will lay the people low. Foreign enemies in war[4] and captivity[5] will complete the ruin of Israel. The destruction will be absolute.[6]

Nowhere does the contrast between Amos and his contemporaries appear more strongly than in the idea of the Day of Yahweh. Israel was looking for some final and supernatural revelation of her God in supreme power, when He should overthrow her enemies and give her all that her heart could desire. In fact, the phrase called up to his mind much what the word " Millennium " does to

---

[1] *Cf.* viii. 13. [2] *Cf.* v. 10. [3] *Cf.* viii. 8. [4] *Cf.* ii. 14, 16, iii. 11, v. 3, vi. 14. etc. [5] *Cf.* v. 27, vi. 7, vii. 17. [6] *Cf.* iii. 12, v. 3, ix. 1-4, etc.

the modern man. To Amos also the Day was to be a revelation; but it was to be a revelation of Yahweh as God of righteousness, not necessarily as God of Israel. And in so far as Israel failed to reach the standard of righteousness, it was to be a day of calamity for her. She would find herself hurried from one danger into a greater, until the final stroke fell upon her, from which there was no recovery.[1] Thus would Yahweh be vindicated, once and for all, by the destruction of that very people whom He had chosen to be His instruments in making Him known to the world. It would seem that the more hopeful tone of ix. 8b-14 is due to a compiler who could not bear the thought of the final destruction of his people, or who knew that a remnant was actually preserved, and so appended a few more optimistic oracles from other, perhaps anonymous, sources. To Amos himself there was practically no hope. Samaria's one chance was to give the moral character of Yahweh its place in her social and religious life.[2] That chance she would not take, and though the final blow was withheld for a generation, it fell in the end as surely as the autumn followed the summer and the summer the spring.

[1] *Cf.* v. 18-20.
[2] *Cf.* v. 6, 14-15.

VII

HOSEA.

A GENERATION passed away, and the doom which had been so real to Amos was still postponed. Yet to an independent observer it must have been clear that it was drawing steadily nearer. The social evils against which the Tekoan prophet had declaimed were only accentuated as time went on. There was in the days of Amos a certain check on the worst forms and expressions of human iniquity in a strong government. It might have been inadequate for such purposes as those of the prophets, but still it was something that kept the free play of men's passion and greed under restraint. But Jeroboam II. was the last of the strong men of the northern kingdom.[1] His death meant the collapse, to a large extent, of the state. Six names after his are given in the list of the Kings of Israel ; one only of these (Menahem) transmitted the throne to his son. The key word to II. Kings xv. (the chapter which records the events of this period) is "conspiracy." One after another men rose and laid violent hands on the crown, not seeing that the very turmoil and confusion of the age made sovereignty in Israel a burden to be feared and a danger to be dreaded. The reign of Zechariah, Jeroboam's

[1] Pekah is possibly an exception, though it is not impossible that we should read "two years" for "twenty years" in II. Ki. xv. 28.

son, is given as six months ; that of his murderer, Shallum,
as one month ; that of Pekahiah, son of Menahem, as
two years. All were assassinated by their successors, as
was also eventually Pekah, the murderer of Pekahiah.

Under such conditions it was inevitable that the general
state of the people should sink lower and lower. It was
no longer a case of the misuse of law and of legitimate
authority ; what the last generation of the northern
kingdom had to bear was the more or less complete absence
of law and authority. Though Menahem, Pekah, and
Hoshea succeeded in maintaining their position for longer
periods,[1] any security that their reigns may have given
was temporary and uncertain. Further, foreign interference, especially that of Assyria, became the rule. All
three of the kings just mentioned were tributary to
Nineveh, and the withholding of tribute was sure to lead
to one of the cruel raids which were the Assyrians' normal
method of securing the allegiance of the various parts
of their heterogeneous empire. It is probable, too, that
it was the fear of such raids that kept Israel loyal to their
own kings. So far had she fallen from the great days
when Ahab and Benhadad had checked the tide of Assyrian
power on the deadly field of Karkar.[2]

It is conditions of this kind that are reflected in the work
of Hosea. He may well be excused for seeing in the institu-
tion of monarchy itself an act of apostasy. Certainly the
repeated political assassination appealed to him as being
utterly inconsistent with the principles of Yahweh—

---

[1] The figures given in the Hebrew Text. of II. Kings are : Menahem, 10
years ; Pekah, 20 years ; and Hoshea, 9 years.   But the transmission of figures in ancient documents is notoriously uncertain,
and dates are difficult to ascertain with accuracy. Thus Jeroboam's
death is by some assigned to 763 B.C., by others to 743.   The
one is probably too early, the other certainly too late.

[2] B.C. 853.   There is no allusion to this event in the Old Testament,
and our knowledge of Ahab's share in the campaign is derived from
Assyrian sources.

" They have made kings, but not by me, princes, and I took no cognisance thereof."[1] Even when established on the throne, these usurpers were of no value to the body politic. They tossed like splinters on the surface of the water,[2] they rose only to fall at once.[3] And a power based on falsehood and treachery[4] could command neither obedience nor respect.[5] Almost as terrible to a patriot was the appeal to Assyria or Egypt.[6] It was no remedy for the manifold diseases that afflicted the nation.[7] On the contrary, it was not merely futile but dangerous,[8] and would sooner or later end in complete ruin.[9] If Israel were to find salvation at all, she must find it in herself, and in any case it was not to be sought in political action but in a genuine moral revolution.

Hence the reader notices one striking difference between the outlook of Amos and that of Hosea. The former has much to say about social and commercial iniquity—the latter relatively little. This is not due to the fact that the life of Israel had undergone any improvement. On the contrary, it was so much worse that it seemed impossible to dwell on details of injustice. The impression made on the observer was that yet more hopeless one in which he is dazed and oppressed by the shapeless and disordered confusion of iniquity, by the stifling farrago of crime.[10] Amos does not condemn the system as a system, because he believes that it is workable if handled in the right spirit ; Hosea does not condemn the system, because to all intents and purposes a system has ceased to exist. It is not hope of the purification of the national life but the fact of its disintegration that is responsible for the prophet's comparative silence.

---

[1] viii. 4. The Hebrew word for " know " connotes far more than the English one, implying an acceptance and a sense of responsibility as well as mere acquaintance with the facts.
[2] x. 7.   [3] vii. 7.   [4] vii. 3.   [5] x. 3.   [6] viii. 9, x. 6.   [7] v. 13.
[8] xii. 1-2.   [9] xi. 10.   [10] iv. 1-4, xi. 12, xii. 7.

Like Amos, however, Hosea stands for a supremely moral conception of Yahweh. Yet he reached his position in a widely different fashion. The older prophet seems to have been a man who had inherited the tradition of a purer faith, and had not lost it by too close a contact with the higher civilisation of Canaan. Hosea's illumination had come in another and more terrible way, through his own tragic experience of love and suffering.

It would seem that the book as we now have it was compiled from two small collections, one of them very short, comprising, in fact, only the first two chapters. At the head of each of these collections was placed an account of Hosea's marriage and its sequel. Ch. i., the first account, tells the story in the third person, just as a good deal of the life of Jeremiah is told for us by one of his friends. The other, briefer, and if possible, more poignant narrative— that of chap. iii.—comes from the prophet's own lips. It is not easy to construct a consistent story from the two, and there have been students of the Old Testament who have preferred to regard ch. iii. as allegorical rather than historical.[1] But the suggestion just given will probably account for the discrepancies that may be met with, and it may be assumed that the two stories refer to the same set of events, the one being written from the outside and the other from the inside.

Both narratives indicate that Hosea received a direct command from Yahweh to marry a harlot. So repulsive is the thought to modern ideas, and so much more repulsive does it seem to have been to the ancient Hebrew mind, that it is generally assumed that this was a deduction from later experience. Gomer, it is supposed, may have been an innocent girl up to the time of her marriage, or if this were not the case it is possible that Hosea was ignorant of her real character. But in face of what we know of the nature of the prophetic inspiration,

[1] *e.g.,* Marti.

and of the extravagant symbolical actions which were
from time to time imposed on the prophets (though the
episode of Isaiah's walking barefoot, or Jeremiah's girdle,
or the numerous acts recorded of Ezekiel, do not in any way
recall or suggest such a procedure as this of Hosea's),
it is not impossible that this was a genuine command
received in the ecstatic state, and that Hosea carried it
out with full knowledge of what he was doing. Further,
it may well be that the intense feeling against sexual
immorality which is so marked a feature of Israelite
psychology might admit of one exception, or at least
palliation. It is a normal feature of polytheistic religious
systems, especially when based on some form of nature-
worship, that sacramental fornication should be included
amongst its rites. This is so in India to-day, it was so in
the later Græco-Roman religion (at least after its contact
with Asiatic cults), and the existence of the practice in
the syncretistic faith of Israel is evidenced by the fact
that one of the Hebrew words for " harlot " is literally
" holy woman." It also seems to have prevailed amongst
others of the more highly civilised Semitic peoples. Now
it may well be that it was felt to be permissible to purchase
such a woman from the shrine to which she was attached,
and to retain her as a wife. It is even conceivable that a
certain religious sanctity attached to such a marriage,
and that the action of the husband was regarded as meri-
torious. Whilst this is pure conjecture, we know of nothing
in the customs and views of ancient Samaria which would
invalidate it, and it would go far to offer a psychological
explanation of the development of Hosea's religious
thought.

It is quite possible that he recognised that her second [1]
and third children were not his. That is suggested

---

[1] The name given to the third child seems to support this view. In the
case of the second it is less probable, but still possible, that Hosea
knew he was not the father.

by the phraseology of the story, and still more clearly in
the names which were given. But it is also true that
though the old life had claimed her in some degree, and
she was unable to resist tendencies implanted in her
by her experience, she was yet allowed to retain a
position in Hosea's household. It is equally clear from all
his passionate language that he loved her. He was a man
possessed and dominated by his love. It went to the very
roots of his being, and so fully did it absorb him that no
sin or folly on her part could shake it. It was no mere
explosive flash of strong emotion that had kindled in his
life, it was a consuming fire shut up in his bones, which
no rejection could weaken and no suffering quench. In
all the world's literature there is no record of human love
like his.

And, being what he was, he knew from his own experience
that there is no true love apart from pain. It may almost
be said that the converse is true, that there is no pain of
the deepest kind without love. The ability to endure is
the test of the capacity for love, and its fuller and richer
development is to be attained only through suffering. To
Christian thought this is as true of Divine love as it is of
human, and in his dim foreshadowing of the supreme revelation of the love of God in the Cross, Hosea contributed a
thought to the world's knowledge of God the influence
and importance of which it is impossible to overrate.

So, as the message of Amos may be summed up in the
word "Justice," that of Hosea may be said to be "Love."
It is true that the more prominent form which love took
in his mind was that of the husband for his wife, but that
was not the only one. One of the most touching and tender
passages in Hebrew literature is that with which ch. xi.
opens. Yahweh is the father of Israel, teaching the child
to walk, and sustaining the toddling steps by holding
the arms. But it is the other which is the more frequent
in the book. The Prophet found his image of the love of

God for man in the holiest of all human relationships, that which more than any other involves at its highest the consecration of one personality to another. So one feels that Hosea has, after all, through his own bitter agony, reached deeper than any other of the Prophets into the secret of religion. For if personality is the ultimate power and the supreme fact in the universe—as it surely is—then it would seem to follow that the supreme experience must be friendship. And the highest mode of friendship will be that in which the mutual surrender of body, mind and spirit is most perfectly demanded. This, on the purely human plane, can be achieved in all its fullness only in marriage. But there is a yet greater form of it, greater because it involves the greatest of all personalities, that of God Himself. And Hosea saw that the coping stone can only be placed on human experience when that highest mode of friendship is carried to its ultimate degree in the love of God.

One effect of this point of view is to be seen in the Prophet's conception of sin. Sin is always an ugly thing, but nowhere—save in the Cross itself—is it made to appear more utterly horrible and loathsome than in the thought of Hosea. To him it is the rejection, or still worse, the betrayal of love. All that God Himself has to give His people He has given. Yahweh, and not the Baals, as men thought, is the source of all material prosperity.[1] It was Yahweh who brought Israel out of Egypt, though from the first they and their ancestors seemed to be unworthy of His care.[2] Yet Israel had taken all too readily to the worship of the gods of Canaan, and Hosea had the insight which could pierce the veil of syncretism and see that the honour paid in name to Yahweh was in reality offered to those old gods—on every high hill, and under every green tree.[3] Thus, whilst Hosea has the same message

[1] ii. 10.   [2] xi. 1. ix. 10. xii. 4. xiii. 5-7.   [3] iv. 12. 13.

in essence as Amos, he carries it deeper. With the earlier
Prophet what is required is mainly right conduct, the right
attitude to man. In the thinking of his great successor,
the right attitude to man is impossible without the right
attitude to God.

All the circumstances of his life tended to reinforce this
position. The contrast in tone between Amos and Hosea
has often been noted, and the comparatively cold enthusiasm
of the one for justice set alongside of the passionate
heart-cry of the other for love. It is clear that one element
in the difference is to be found in the man's domestic
sorrow. But there is another. Amos came to Bethel from
the outside, and the true meaning of the life of Samaria
was brought home to him by the contrast it presented to
the simpler and purer society and religion he had always
known.[1] Hosea was a man of the city. Many of his
analogies and figures are drawn from the life of the towns-
man. His most striking figures of speech seem to have been
drawn from the bakehouse[2]—is it possible that he was a
baker by trade ? And his acquaintance with the political
gossip of the day has already been noted. All this meant
that he was himself inextricably bound up with the sins
and fortunes of his own people. It is to be remembered
that the idea of individual religion was yet to be born.
A man could not stand apart from his own folk in responsibility. He might see where they were wrong, and might
do all that lay in his power to attract or to drive them into
right courses. But he could not escape in any degree from
personal complicity in their misdeeds. The truest of all
patriots is he who, like Hosea (and Jeremiah after him),
identifies himself with his people, sorrows over her calamities

[1] The view of Prof. Welch and others that Amos was really a native
of the northern kingdom (*Religion of Israel under the Monarchy*)
though interesting and important, is hardly borne out by the tone
of the book itself.
[2] *Cf.* vii. 6, 8.

as though they were his own, and repents for her sins as
though he had committed them himself. It is this sense
of bitter personal remorse, unexpressed but latent in every
line, that runs as an undercurrent through all the message
of Hosea, and adds to the tenderness of the whole, and,
perhaps, helps him to go deeper than any other into the
spiritual needs of his time.

For he saw that the lack of love in the heart of Israel
was due to the fact that they simply did not know Yahweh.[1]
This may imply in part that they did not consider Him in
their actions. But it is equally true that to the mind of
Hosea they were ignorant of their God in the ordinary sense
of the word. You cannot love a person with whom you are
not acquainted in any way. And Israel utterly failed to
recognise in any way that Yahweh was different from
the Baals. The Prophet knew better. He could see that
in trying to worship Yahweh as men worshipped other
gods, they were not really worshipping Him at all, but
those others whom they affected to disown. Had they
known what He was really like, there would have been
no danger of their making the appalling errors they did
make. They would not have credited the other gods with
the production of corn and wine and oil. They would not
even have supposed that because Yahweh could do what
the Baals did, He therefore desired to be worshipped as
the Baals were. Whilst we should probably not be justified
in drawing a parallel between the teaching of Hosea
and that attributed to Socrates, this much must be
admitted, both alike are right in insisting that men have
little chance of doing what is right unless they can recognise
it. And, as already noted in discussing the attitude of Amos,
the trouble was not that men did not know right from wrong.
This they did know, and seem to have been not unwilling
to apply their knowledge to the affairs of everyday life.

---

[1] *Cf.* iv. 1, 6, 11 ; v. 4 ; vii. 11.

The real difficulty lay in the fact that they did not attribute to their God the same moral ideals as they held for themselves. They supposed Him to be interested in ritual, in worship, and in sacrifice, and failed to realise that He was in truth the champion and guardian of those very principles of right which they accepted in private life.

It seems almost certain that this truth was brought home to Hosea by the tragedy of his home life. If, as has been suggested, his wife was originally a sacred prostitute, her former life might be condoned. But when, after marriage and after bearing to her husband a son, she resumed the habits of the heathen réligieuse, the contrast and the incongruity would at once become obvious. To the agonised lover the thing became immeasurably horrible—the more horrible because he still loved her with the old passion. But after all, he must have reflected, it was only what she had been doing before his purchase of her, and doing in the ostensible service of Yahweh. If the thing was horrible now, it followed that it must have been not less horrible then. It is not an accident that the most common metaphor for apostasy in this book is fornication.[1] It is not a mere metaphor, but an accurate and terrible description of an actual feature in the religious life of Israel. This leaves the thoughtful man with a dilemma. Either Yahweh who demands this thing is morally worse than the man who loathes it, or men are mistaken in supposing that Yahweh really demands it. To Hosea the former position would have appealed as a complete subversion of his faith, and he was left with the other alternative—the worship of Israel was at least as terrible in the sight of Yahweh as it was in the sight of His Prophet. In that case Israel must have utterly misunderstood her God—she was perishing for lack of knowledge.

A further evil in this practice was that it reacted on men's

[1] *Cf.* i. 2, ii. 2-5 ; iv. 12, 15, 18 ; v. 3, 4 ; ix. 1.

appreciation of Yahweh. Because they had so misunderstood Him, they had given way to this form of iniquity, and this in turn made the acquisition of true knowledge of Him impossible. Indulgence in sin, especially of the grosser sort, has this extra danger, that it deludes the mind and dulls the conscience. Because of the thing itself they could not see that it was wrong.[1] What they needed, if it were only possible to them, was to get away from the stupefying contact with sin and look at it from a detached point of view. Then they would be able to see what it was really like. Implicated in it, steeped in it, wallowing in it, they were *ipso facto* incapable of forming a judgment.

Another form of vice, also practised apparently in Canaanite worship, was drunkenness. The vine was a typical product of the agricultural community. As such it was always held to stand in a special relation to the gods of tillage—*i.e.*, the Baals. When Yahweh was reduced to the level of a Baal, it was not unnatural that this special relationship should be transferred to Him also. There is reason to suspect that in some forms of Canaanite religion wine was used to stimulate the prophetic ecstasy, and from the words of Amos it is clear that it was employed in certain rites in the Temple at Bethel.[2] To Hosea, liberated from the deadening conviction that whatever was was right, intoxication appeared only disgusting.[3] As in the case of Amos, we may fairly note how far the Prophet was ahead of the Nazirite. The latter objected to the use of wine on grounds of traditional religious conventionality. His protest was in a sense symbolical. In this he is typical of the ancient world. It is only in comparatively recent times that there has been any movement against the use of wine on moral grounds, and even actual drunkenness has not always been regarded as a serious blot on conduct. But

---

[1] iv. 11, where the mention of fornication is, however, suspected by some moderns.
[2] Am. ii. 8. *Cf.* also Hos. ix. 4.   [3] ix. 2.

Hosea's position is much nearer to that of the modern temperance reformer. He challenges the use of alcohol, not because of its religious associations, but because of its practical effects. Like sexual vice, it tends to destroy men's thinking powers.[1] It militates against intellectual efficiency, and thereby renders men incapable of thinking straight. To his mind, one of the reasons why Israel does not know Yahweh is that her brains are fuddled, and though the protest is not elaborated—Hosea has less to say on the subject than Isaiah has—his occasional references leave no doubt as to his views and motives.

This ignorance extended to other elements in the worship of Israel, though it is still the main line of Hosea's thought and dominates him when his mind turns to the cultus. He feels as if the whole of the worship of Israel were permeated by this moral rottenness.[2] It would almost seem as if sacrifice itself in Hosea's eyes were wicked.[3] But more striking is his protest against the worship of the calf or bull at Bethel. This marks a real advance in religious thought. Whatever Amos felt, he has left no record of an objection to idolatry, and the accounts of earlier times which have been handed down to us have been largely coloured by the later theology which held all idolatry to be a form of apostasy. The narratives of the patriarchs, and indeed of the first few kings, occasionally contain references which have escaped the hands of the orthodox editors, and show that the representation of Yahweh in some material form was far from being objectionable. Though the traditional epithet attached to the name of Jeroboam ben Nebat is " who made Israel to sin," it is practically certain that in the cultus attributed to him there was no conscious deviation from the will of Yahweh.

[1] *Cf.* iv 11.
[2] *Cf.* vi. 10, where " Bethel " seems to be the right reading instead of " House of Israel."
[3] *Cf.* viii. 11.

But here Hosea goes further than any of his predecessors.
One must, of course, beware of attributing to him a conception of Yahweh like our modern view of God. It is by
no means clear that he started from the point of view of
pure spirituality, and therefore realised that idolatry was,
to put it mildly, insulting to Yahweh. The contrary appears
to have been the case. His bitter hatred of the whole of
the Bethel cultus led him to question the form in which
Yahweh was presented. One cannot be sure that the same
protest would have arisen had Hosea been face to face
with the serpent-worship of Jerusalem. But the bull has
nearly always had phallic associations, and there may have
been elements in the actual ritual which brought this out.[1]
If that be so, it was inevitable that the man's holy rage
should fall upon the thing that was the sign and emblem
of that feature in the erroneous worship of Israel which his
own soul's story had taught him to detest most completely.

Hence Hosea's denunciations of the worship of the "calf,"
and his threats of its destruction.[2] But he did not stop
there. He does seem to have realised that it was impossible
to represent Yahweh, the mighty God who had brought
Israel out of Egypt, under any material form whatever.
It is clear that he did condemn the making of an idol of
any kind,[3] and so prepared the way for the clearer message
which rang out in Israel before the return from the Exile.

Such an error in worship exhibited a fatal ignorance of
Yahweh. But that ignorance was, if possible, even more
conspicuous in Israel's failure to understand the meaning
of repentance. It must not be supposed that she had no
conception of sin at all, that she always supposed that she

---

[1] It is, of course, possible that serpent-worship contained a phallic
element, but it is significant that no protest against it on Isaiah's
part has been recorded.

[2] *Cf.* viii. 5, 6, and possibly x. 5.

[3] *Cf.* viii. 4, xiii. 2-4. Only the " molten image " is expressly mentioned,
but the condemnation would apply equally to the " graven image."

was maintaining the full favour of Yahweh. She was only too ready to attribute her calamities to His wrath, and to seek the best means whereby that wrath might be appeased. Her failure lay in her inability to realise what it was that was cutting her off from her God, and was rousing Him to act against her Still less did she see how she should humble herself before Him, and what measures she should adopt to secure a return of His favour. She took too easy a view of His character. She supposed that a verbal admission of the fact that she had done wrong would be sufficient, that a mild remedy would cure her sickness. She thought of Yahweh as loving her, and believed that she could exploit His love.[1] A few extra sacrifices, a fast or two, a special day of national humiliation and prayer—these, she fancied, would suffice. But they would not suffice. She must go right down to the roots of things, and see that it was her whole outlook on life, her whole view of the character of Yahweh that was at fault. He had no need of sacrifice. He was not to be cajoled by a special helping at a common meal. He was not to be bought even by the complete consecration of slaughtered victims, whose bodies were wholly consumed upon the altar. It was an absolute moral revolution that He required, a completely new attitude towards God and man that was the *sine qua non* with Him. The other was too shallow and too evanescent—early dew or morning cloud, and the very misunderstanding thereby exhibited would make the doom of the sinful people only the surer.

For Yahweh was essentially a God of principle and not a God of whim. He stood behind all phenomena and all causation. The laws of material and physical reaction are, as far as we know, invariable. Equally so, could we but see them as clearly as the Prophet could, are the laws of the

---

[1] vi. 1-6. The meaning and originality of this passage have been disputed, but the probability is that G. A. Smith's interpretation is the right one.

moral and spiritual world. It is true that the forgiveness
of God is free, but that forgiveness never consists in
" letting the culprit off." " Whatsoever a man soweth,
that shall he also reap " is a doctrine which had gripped
Hosea centuries before Paul stated it in those words.[1]
No man can escape from the consequences of his own
deeds. When we say that God punishes, we must remember
that there is no arbitrary or chance method whereby the
judgment is apportioned. The flagrant immorality of the
men of Israel could only result in parallel behaviour on
the part of the women, breaking up the purity and sanctity
of home life. And the responsibility would rest with
the men, not merely with the women.[2] But there was also
this to be noted : whilst the crop must be of the same kind
as the seed, it would be inevitably larger in volume and in
force. " Some thirty, some sixty, some a hundredfold,"
would be necessarily true of Israel's conduct, as well as
of natural products. She might sow a gentle breeze ; what
she reaped would be a hurricane.

So Israel was doomed. She had sown her seed and must
abide the certain growth of her crop. There are passages
in the book as it now stands which seem to hold out promise
of a brighter future, but doubts have been raised by
some scholars as to whether any of these can be attributed
to Hosea himself.[3]   Almost every conceivable mage of
destruction is invoked. Moth and mildew, corrupting in
slow silence,[4] the raging sword and the savage beast—all
would be employed against her. For Yahweh is not a man
that He should go back on His word.[5] What He has said
stands ; what Israel has done will inevitably meet with
its own reward. Yet He loves His own child, and her doom
is almost more than He can bear.[6] A lesser love than

---

[1] viii. 7, x. 13.   [2] Cf. iv. 14.
[3] For the opposite view cf. Melville Scott : The Message of Hosea.
[4] Cf. v. 8-14.   [5] Cf. xi. 9, to be read as a question : "Shall I not—"
[6] Cf. xi. 8 (the originality of the verse is suspected by some editors).

Yahweh's would have given way and spared her, and that would have been a cruel kindness. For there are circumstances in which it is better that a people should cease to exist than that they should go on as they are. In such case is Israel, and He who loves her loves her enough even to destroy her—though His own heart utterly break with the blow.[1]

But that is not the end. For Hosea, like Jeremiah after him, was an optimist of that type which cannot believe in the final victory of evil. Punishment would fall, and it would seem final. But there would be another chance. Once again Yahweh would come to Israel and woo her. Once again He would bring her to the valley of Achor, that defile up which Joshua had passed from the plain of Jericho. And this time it would be a door of hope.[2] Hosea could speak yet more strongly. Though the child perish in the womb and come still-born into the world, He could and would give it life.[3] At long last, Love must win, for God is Love.

---

[1] *Cf.* xi. 1.-8.   [2] ii. 15.   [3] viii. 13 *f.*

VIII

JUDEAN PROPHETS OF THE EIGHTH CENTURY :
MICAH AND ISAIAH

THE age which saw the ruin and deportation of Samaria
was not without its special importance in the political
world for the sister kingdom in the South. One gathers
that the general social conditions, with their moral implications, were much the same there as in the North. The
countrymen found the same difficulty in securing justice
from the legal authorities. There was the same spirit of
greed manifested amongst the landed classes. There was,
perhaps, less blatant luxury ; but if this were so, it was due
to lack of opportunity rather than to a deeper spirituality.
There were similar complaints as to the character and
honesty of the leaders, civil and religious, except for the
fact that the central government appears to have been
at once somewhat stronger and somewhat purer. It is a
striking fact that Isaiah is to be found acting in co-operation
with his sovereign rather than in hostility to him. The
greatest difference in the positions of the two states was
presented by their respective situations in relation to foreign
peoples. Judah seems to have been to a large extent a
mere appendage of Israel during this period. Smaller
and more insignificant than her neighbour, she at once
missed the advantages and avoided the dangers of Samaria.

She had comparatively little contact with the world outside her own borders. Samaria was on the main trade route which connected Asia with Africa. It was this which, on the weakening of the Syrian hostility, brought wealth and material prosperity to her people. Jerusalem was a little hill state, which never seems to have reached out as far as the Mediterranean coast. The great road, along which the merchandise of all the ages has moved, runs through the gap formed by Esdraelon in the Palestinian central range, and passes down the maritime plain, leaving Judah and Jerusalem away to the east behind the foothills. The world's traffic tended thus to pass her by. But at the same time, that position which was so advantageous to Samaria commercially proved in the end to be her ruin. For it was inevitable that in the long run the great African power—Egypt—and the great Asiatic power—in this case Assyria—should find in her a " buffer state." With the ambition of conquest stronger than the fear of an enemy, the instinct of each was to seize and try to absorb this small country, and so to win a step nearer to the goal of world dominion. But Jerusalem lay to one side, and provided that she refrained from meddling in the affairs of other nations, the great armies of Assyria and Egypt could pass her by and leave her untouched while they aimed at a nobler foe. It is this in part which explains the survival of Jerusalem for nearly a century and a half after the fall of Samaria, and it is a noteworthy fact that whenever Judah was seriously invaded by either of the two great powers, the first act of hostility seems to have come from herself.

The work of two Prophets of this period in the south has come down to us—Micah and Isaiah. Both seem to have been younger contemporaries of Hosea. The extant oracles of the former have been preserved for us in the book which bears his name, though there is much other matter bound up with them. It is now widely held that the prophecies of Micah proper end with iii. 12, and there

have been added to them two smaller collections of anonymous work, comprised in chs. iv.-v. and vi.-vii. respectively.
The exact date of these collections is uncertain ; apparently
both contain material by different authors and from
different periods.[1]   For Micah himself it is necessary to
rely on chs. i.-iii.

The prophet was a native of the lower hills between the
central range and the maritime plain. The circumstances
and conditions have been strikingly and adequately
described by G. A. Smith,[2] and it is clear that Micah
himself had all the strength and the weakness that such a
locality as this would be likely to breed. His horizon is
small ; he does not seem even to mention Assyria. His
vision is limited in the main to the group of villages sur-
rounding his country home. It is the sorrows and the
injustice experienced by the peasant farmer which arouses
his bitter indignation, and of the luxury and wickedness
of the big city he has little or nothing to say. But he is
intense, passionate, uncompromising, with that same clear
vision as to the difference between right and wrong which
characterised Amos. In one respect he seems to go deeper
than the latter, inasmuch as he sees that the evil which
was crushing the life out of the countryside was the
avarice of the country magnates,[3] and not merely the
judicial corruption which gave that avarice its chance.[4]
He has imagination. He can call up a fine picture of the
grand entry of Yahweh into the arena of Judah's life,[5]
and her destruction is described with vigour and even with
violence of language. He has a striking habit of playing
upon words, especially proper names. This tendency is
found elsewhere in Hebrew literature, but is nowhere so
prominent as in Micah.

---

[1] The mixed character of these collections makes it difficult to give them
separate treatment.   Attention has been called to the two most
important passages, iv. 1-4 and vi. 6-8.

[2] Hist. Geog. of Holy Land, pp. 207-209.   [3] *Cf.* ii. 1-10

[4] Not that he is blind to this—*cf.* iii. 1, 9.   [5] *Cf.* i. 3-5.

As the Prophet sees the social life of his community, there is hardly an element in it that is not rotten right through. It is true that he has nothing to say about the king, but no words are too strong to describe the iniquities of the "country gentry." We see through his powerful and dramatic speech their passion for expanding their estates—with calculating violence towards the rightful owners[1]—and the forced labour by which they built their homes.[2] These men—one is reminded of Hosea's complaint of the ignorance of Yahweh's people—*ought* to have known what the will of Yahweh was, and where justice lay. But they positively hated goodness and loved evil, "skinning" the countryside and devouring the very flesh of the peasants.[3] It is interesting to note that there seems to be no condemnation of the cultus in itself; Micah is no more concerned to set up a system of worship than was Amos. But the professed religious people had little enough to recommend them personally. Prophets, Seers, and Diviners, together with the priesthood, are using their office and their gifts merely to secure their own material prosperity.[4]

Against all this the soul of the Prophet rises up in protest. True, he does in some measure feel the horror of the punishment which will fall upon Judah and her rulers,[5] but not as Hosea feels it. In the main he is so occupied with the contemplation of men's sin, that he has little sympathy to spare for their suffering. The result is that his words burn with revolutionary ardour, and he longs at all costs to see that the iniquitous rich are overthrown and justice is done.

Micah does not rely on the human weapons of the revolutionary. He insists that Yahweh will reveal himself to his people,[6] and when He does so it will be to punish Judah's sin. For that is the only possible issue, and Judah is rushing towards it at her highest speed. And his words

---

[1] *Cf.* ii. 1-3. [2] *Cf.* iii. 10. [3] *Cf.* iii. 2-3. [4] *Cf.* iii. 11.
[5] *Cf.* i. 8-9. [6] *Cf.* i. 3-5.

found some echo in the conscience of his people, and a century later it was remembered that he had given warning and that men had staved off punishment by timely and thorough repentance.[1]

Yet Micah is only a peasant, with the peasant's experience and the peasant's outlook. Whilst he reminds one in some ways of Amos, he stands on a far lower level of importance. One cannot tell what would have been his message had he been brought into sudden contact with the complicated city life as was his great predecessor ; but there is nothing in his extant work which would indicate that he would have reached the same heights or have taken the same position in the growth of man's knowledge of God. Nevertheless God used him, and used him so effectively that, in the generations immediately following, his message seems to have created a far deeper impression than that of a man whom later ages have acclaimed as one of the greatest of spiritual teachers whom the race has known.

For God uses great men as well as small, and in Isaiah the son of Amoz He employed one of His noblest instruments. It is true that much which former generations used to attribute to him is no longer regarded as being from his lips. We have now reason to believe that there is nothing after ch. xxxix. of the book which bears his name which is in any way connected with him. It would seem that two later collections of oracles were accidentally appended to an original Book of Isaiah, one (chs. xl.-lv.) dating from the last years of the Exile, the other (chs. lvi.-lxvi.), due mainly to prophets whose activity is to be placed somewhere in the half century preceding the coming of Nehemiah to Jerusalem. Even in chs. i.-xxxix. there is a good deal which is now not usually assigned to Isaiah himself. This involves no denial of its inspiration or of

[1] *Cf.* Jeremiah xxvi. 18-19.

its value as divine revelation, for it is no longer believed
that God is limited in His choice of servants to certain
named individuals. Nor is there any attempt in the modern
position to belittle the literary power of the inspired
unknowns. In fact, some of the greatest pieces of writing
in the whole book are included amongst these anonymous
writings. Such, for instance, is the great taunt-song over
the fall of the tyrant in Is. xiv. Other portions regarded
as anonymous are chs. xi.-xii., xxi. 1-12, xxiv.-xxvii., xxx.
18-26, xxxiii.-xxxv. Some of these passages carry the stamp
of the Exile, others reflect the conditions of the restored
Israel. One short section—ii. 2-4—seems to have been a
floating anonymous oracle, which was also prefixed to
the second collection included in the Book of Micah,
and may have been older or younger than either. The
small collections which were ultimately built into the
present book are fairly well marked. Ch. i. is introductory
to the whole, and may include some of the latest of
Isaiah's utterances, since there are verses which seem
to refer to the invasion of Sennacherib in 701. Chs.
ii.-v. clearly formed a booklet of Isaianic material. So also
chs. vi.-xii., including later appendices in xi. and xii.
Chs. xiii.-xxiii. are mainly concerned with foreign nations—
the tendency to group together such oracles appears in other
books as well—and xxiv.-xxvii. form a great Apocalypse,[1]
independent and self-contained. Chs. xxviii.-xxxv.[2] consist
of woes pronounced on certain forms of sin, intermingled
with the promise of a better time to come, and xxxvi.-xxxix.
are a historical appendix which finds a parallel in large
measure in the Book of Kings. Details can be studied in
any standard Introduction, such as that of Driver or of Gray.

Yet even the narrowing down of the sources from which
our knowledge of this prophet is derived has done his
reputation and his greatness little if any harm. What is

[1] See Ch. XIV.   [2] The greater part of xxviii.-xxxi. and possibly
other portions are to be regarded as Isaiah's own work.

still universally attributed to him reveals him as one of
the grandest figures of all time. In the rediscovery of the
Bible, which marked the religious life of the nineteenth
century, he was hailed as a man who stood head and
shoulders above his contemporaries as a statesman.
To-day there is a tendency to dispute this claim. As a matter
of fact its justice depends on the meaning imported into
the word. If it is supposed to imply that his instinct was
to look on life from the point of view of the international
politician, then it may be difficult to maintain the position.
There is nothing in Isaiah's writings to suggest that he sat
down carefully to consider the geographical situation of
his people amidst the nations of the world, that he
appreciated the historical significance of the movements
of armies and of the ambitions of monarchs, and that he
based his " political " utterances on cold calculations of
population, man-power, or economic resources.

But, at the same time, it is impossible to deny to Isaiah
an extraordinarily wide range of interests. He was alive
to all the great political factors of his day. Assyria and
Egypt were beyond the horizon of Micah. To Amos they
were distant nations, possibly dangerous, but still remote.
To Hosea they were imminent perils, threatening the life
of the nation, and vainly invoked as substitutes for God.
To Isaiah they were gigantic world-powers, playing their
part in the evolution of human history, as Israel must play
hers. It would seem that the prophet was familiar with the
court—otherwise it is difficult to explain his dealings with
both Ahaz and Hezekiah. And certainly he had the wide
horizon and the universal outlook (as far as the world was
yet known) without which no politician can ever rise to
the level of statesmanship. To him the further nations
were real and significant.

But—and it is here that he parts company with the mere
statesman—the significance of these nations lay in the fact
that they were all related to a higher and more fully

dominant principle, the will of Yahweh. It would probably be an illicit deduction from the facts to ascribe a pure monotheism to Isaiah, but he did feel, like Amos before him, that Yahweh was concerned with the fortunes of the whole human race, and not merely with those of Israel. Thus he developed a genuine philosophy of history, and conceived all events to be subordinated to the working out of a single sublime plan. That plan is itself the vindication and illustration of supreme moral laws, which to him are summed up in the character of Yahweh. There are " laws " in the physical world whose operation is absolute. Just as absolute and just as inevitable are the human phenomena which result from the ethical and spiritual laws in which the will of the "Holy One of Israel" is enshrined and expressed. Hence it follows that though Assyria may believe herself to be a free agent, she is as a matter of fact simply the weapon which Yahweh uses to avenge the breach of His laws on the corrupt and rotting civilisation of the western world.[1] Should she fail to realise this truth, she in turn will have it brought home to her in disaster whose magnitude is only to be measured by the power which she has previously wielded.[2]

We must glance briefly at the story of the events in which Isaiah thus saw the guiding hand of God. The date commonly assigned to the beginning of his ministry is 740, almost the *terminus ad quem* for the period of Hosea's activity. In 736 it would seem that an attempt was made by Pekah of Samaria and Rezin of Damascus to resist further Assyrian encroachment in the West. It appeared to them to be imperative that Judah should at least be neutral, and they therefore attempted to secure her adherence, either by making a treaty with Ahaz or by placing an Aramean on his throne. Having no hope of a single-handed resistance to such a coalition (which

[1] *Cf.* Is. x. 5, 6.   [2] *Cf.* Is. x. 7-11, 24-26, etc.

probably had Egypt behind it) he appealed to Assyria.
His action was superfluous ; Assyria would have interfered
in any case. In 734 Damascus was captured and destroyed,
whilst Samaria was only allowed to continue a separate
existence under the government of an Assyrian nominee,
Hoshea. But the empire of Nineveh was only held
together by the personality of her reigning sovereign, and
the death of Tiglath-Pileser roused fresh hopes of autonomy
throughout his dominions.[1] His successors, Shalmaneser
and Sargon, however, were no weaklings, and not many
years passed before Assyrian armies were in Palestine.
Samaria fell in 722, and was never again the capital of an
independent state. The real Assyrian objective, however,
was now as always Egypt, and the slow southern movement
of the Mesopotamian power was illustrated by Sargon's
capture of Ashdod in 711. But what Egypt could not do
by force of arms, she did by intrigue, and when Sennacherib
succeeded Sargon, the whole of the West was in a blaze.
Practically all the states of Palestine and the neighbouring
country were nominally attached to Assyria, and ruled
by princes who owed allegiance to Nineveh. All revolted,
with a single exception. The only Assyrian vassal who
remained faithful to his suzerain was one Padi, king of
Ekron. The rebel princes, with Egypt behind them,
acted in concert. Aided by a revolution within the city,
they took Ekron, and imprisoned Padi. Looking
round for a suitable place in which to detain him,
they fixed upon Jerusalem, probably because it was felt
to be one of the least exposed of the Palestinian cities,
and the captive prince was committed in chains to Hezekiah
for safe keeping. But it was not long before Sennacherib
was on the spot to vindicate his authority. He swept
Palestine with fire and sword. His own record states that
he captured forty-six fortified cities in Judah alone, and

---

[1] This is perhaps the reference in Is. xiv. 29-32.

carried off hundreds of thousands of the population into slavery But he did not take Jerusalem. He closely invested the city, it is true—" I shut up Hezekiah like a bird in a cage " is his picturesque phrase—but it seems that for once the Egyptians did something effective, and created a diversion in the south which compelled Sennacherib temporarily to raise the siege. What happened after that is not clear, but it is certain that in some way the Assyrian armies suffered an appalling disaster, which was not a military one. It is not impossible that they were attacked by bubonic plague, which had been known in Palestine for at least four centuries. They were so weakened as to make a return to Mesopotamia imperative, though it would seem that they still had the strength to exact a crushing tribute from Hezekiah. So at least Sennacherib says, and whilst any figures he gives are open to suspicion, the essential fact is probably true. It is noteworthy that even he does not claim to have taken Jerusalem, and the miraculous deliverance of the city left a lasting impression on the mind of Judah.

Isaiah, as we have already seen, was far from being indifferent to the political and military events of his time. On many of them he seems to have had something to say and the Book of Kings represents him as one of Hezekiah's advisers. He had only one thing to tell his people. Let Judah refrain from interference, and no harm would befall her.[1] He tried to reassure Ahaz in 736 as to the weakness of the Syro-Ephraimite league, and to dissuade the king from taking any active steps to introduce the Assyrians.[2] But Ahaz would not listen, and the result was dependence on Nineveh which might have been avoided—Ahaz did homage to Tiglath-Pileser at Damascus after the capture of that city in 734. To Ethiopian envoys he would have courteously refused their request for an alliance.[3] But his

---

[1] *Cf.* xxx. 15.   [2] *Cf.* viii. 5-8.   [3] *Cf.* xviii. 1-6.

strongest antipathy was reserved for the intrigues of Egypt. To him the party at the Court who were in favour of Egyptian influence were guilty of disloyalty to Yahweh.[1] He seems to have been also convinced of the political incapacity of the Pharaohs and of their advisers.[2] He foresaw their complete ruin, and more space in this book is given to the doom of Egypt than to that of any other non-Israelite people.[3] The only instance of symbolic action recorded of him has special reference to the fate of that country.[4] Most of the neighbouring tribes were the subjects of his prophecies of destruction. The only apparent exceptions are Edom and Ammon, neither of which is mentioned by name in any passage that we can certainly ascribe to Isaiah. But Philistia,[5] Moab,[6] Damascus,[7] and Tyre,[8] are all threatened with invasion and defeat, together with one or two peoples whose names are obscure, but which were, perhaps, Bedawin tribes from the borders of the desert.[9]

Now it may well be that Isaiah had formed a just estimate of the superior power of Assyria, of the danger of interfering in international politics, and of the futility of challenging the Mesopotamian power. But this was never the principal motive with him. He carried his religion into his politics, and it was his sense of Yahweh that dictated his attitude to all nations. Assyria might have the most powerful military organisation on earth, but Yahweh was stronger than Assyria, and even the " rod of His anger," if she went too far, would find that the God of Israel could protect His own.[10] Still more, then, should Judah have seen that her only true defender and friend was Yahweh. It was safer for her to trust in Him than

---

[1] *Cf.* xxx. 2-3, xxxi. 1-3.   [2] *Cf.* xix. 11-12.   [3] *Cf.* xix., xx., etc.
[4] *Cf.* xx. 3-5.   [5] *Cf.* xiv. 28-32.
[6] *Cf.* xv., xvi., though some of the oracles included are floating anonymous matter.
[7] *Cf.* xvii. 1-3.   [8] *Cf.* xxiii. 1-14.   [9] *Cf.* xvii. 12-14, xxi. 13-17.
[10] *Cf* x. 12, 24-26 ; xiv. 24-27 ; xxx. 31 ; xxxi. 8-9.

even to repair her weak and damaged battlements.[1] Not
only supreme power was His, but supreme wisdom also.
It was worse than useless to exclude Him from the councils
of the nation. He was ready to make Himself known, in
prophecy and in other ways, and there was no need to adopt
any other course than to consult Him under all circumstances.[2] The first thing, the last thing, the only thing
for Israel to remember was that He was her God, and she
His people.[3]

Just as God appealed to Amos as Justice and to Hosea
as Love, so the element in Yahweh's character which came
home with most force to Isaiah was His Holiness. The term
was a familiar one, and implied anything that tended to
appropriate people or things to God. The holy object was
one which was apart from all that was secular, cut off from
profane men and from profane usage. It does not follow,
of course, that there was necessarily any moral content in
the word. Too frequently the exact opposite was the case.
But with Isaiah that ethical conception was fundamental.
A thing might be set apart for a god, but to what could
Yahweh Himself be set apart ? It could be to nothing less
than absolute moral purity, free from spot or defilement.
It must not be forgotten that there still remained in Israel
the memory, and to some extent the standards, of the
higher and simpler ethic of the desert. The problem before
the Prophets was to translate this into terms of the life of
the agricultural community of Palestine. It has already
been remarked that in private life Israel had a really high
conception of right and wrong. Men never wholly lack a
conscience, and it is surprising to find how far they are
at one in the moral judgments they pass on different acts.
But the trouble was that in the syncretistic worship of the
settled Israel, these judgments were not applied to the
practices of the temples and the shrines. To Isaiah it

[1] *Cf.* xxii. 9-11   [2] *Cf.* xxix. 15-24.   [3] *Cf.* xxx. 27-30.

was given to stress and develop that doctrine which Amos had already taught—that Yahweh was Himself far removed from all that men's instincts for purity would regard as foul. Just as Israel was assumed to be consecrated to Him, so He had consecrated Himself to that which was revealed by the highest and the best in humanity. And in so consecrating Himself, He transcended His people, and not merely conformed to her standards of right and wrong, but set up for her high and ever higher ideals to which she might strive.

That moral quality of holiness in Yahweh had come home to Isaiah in the great experience which made him a Prophet. From the day when the ecstasy first fell upon him to the end of his ministry, it was stamped upon his soul. Nothing defiled or unclean could hold communion with that perfect God, and all else must be purged away from Yahweh's people. Yahweh was "the Holy of Israel," and she, in her turn, must be a holy people. This demand expresses itself in many of the applications made by the Prophet's predecessors, and Isaiah repeats not a few of their condemnations. Like them, he saw in calamity a punishment for sin.[1] Like Amos, he found the root of social evils in the selfish luxury of the women,[2] demanded purity and impartiality in the administration of justice,[3] denounced a non-moral ritual,[4] and pleaded for a return to Yahweh.[5] Like Hosea, he deplored the lack of knowledge,[6] and found in the practical polytheism of the country a real apostasy from Yahweh.[7] His passion for agrarian righteousness is at least as strong as that of Micah.[8] Yet he has a quality of his own in presenting these truths. Of all the pre-exilic Prophets he has the most optimistic tone. It has been doubted whether either Amos or Hosea ever had cultivated a real hope of redemption and security, though the

[1] *Cf.* iii. 8 ; xvii. 9-11.   [2] *Cf.* iii. 16 ; iv. 1 ; xxxii. 9-12.
[3] *Cf.* x. 1-4.   [4] *Cf.* i. 10-17 ; xxix. 13-14.   [5] *Cf.* xvii. 7-8.
[6] *Cf.* i. 2-3.   [7] *Cf. e.g.* ii. 6-9 ; xxxi. 6, 7.   [8] *Cf.* v. 8-9.

doubt has itself been challenged; Hosea at any rate stood very near to the fulfilment of the destruction which he foresaw. But the evils of which the Prophets complained seem to have been less virulent in Judah than in the North. The fact that it was under the influence of the Prophets that the reformers of a later generation sought to centralise worship in the capital would seem to involve the acceptance of a higher standard there than prevailed elsewhere.

Be this as it may, Isaiah draws a picture of the future of his people which is by no means so gloomy or so desperate as that of his predecessors and contemporaries. He believed that it was possible that Judah should consider her ways. With faith and hope he summoned her to return to her God.[1] Whilst there would be for the people as a whole the punishment which was inevitably the fruit of sin, there would also be those who should survive and form the nucleus of a really holy nation.[2] This was in a certain sense inevitable from his sense of Yahweh. He needed in Isaiah's days a nation for His own self-expression, and though He might vindicate His character on that very nation, He would yet have to restore her in order to exhibit also His own righteousness and moral holiness to the world.

Such a nation would require for its full development a recognised leader. So it comes to pass that Isaiah's picture of the new time was bound up with a conception which appears in him for the first time in Israelite prophecy— that of the Messiah. Such passages as his exultation over the birth of a young prince[3]—or was it some other child ?— and that which describes the expectation of a king who shall rule in justice[4] indicate the extent of his faith and hope. It is true that if Isaiah had in mind any particular prince born in his own lifetime, that hope was doomed to disappointment, but none the less the principle had been

[1] *Cf.* xvii. 7, 8 ; i. 25-27, etc. [2] *Cf.* x. 20-22, etc.
[3] *Cf.* ix. 6, 7.   [4] xxxii. 1 ff.

laid down. The Christian Church may have been injudicious in her insistence on details, and her method of applying prophecy may at times have been unworthy of the God who inspired it. Nevertheless she has been right in tracing her Messianic doctrine back to the work of Isaiah. For he was the first of the Prophets to give expression to that Divine principle of personal leadership which reached perfection only in the Incarnation of God in Jesus Christ.

IX

THE SEVENTH CENTURY PROPHETS

ONE curious feature of the history of Israel is the way in which our knowledge of different periods varies. There is hardly any time in the history of our own country—at least before the Renaissance—which is better known to us than the history of Israel and Judah in the eighth century B.C. But for the first three-quarters of the seventh century we have to rely on the most meagre notices. This applies not only to the history as given to us in our Old Testament, but also to the sources of information from outside Israel. The period seems to have been covered in the main by the reign of Manasseh, whose devotion to Canaanite practices earned for him the execration of the later writers. From the disaster suffered by Sennacherib in 701 down to the beginning of the last quarter of the century, the historian feels that he is groping in the darkness of a tunnel into which only the faintest light penetrates from its extremities.

Yet great events were happening in the larger world. Assyria had nearly run her long and terrible career of brigandage and of cruelty. The last of her great monarchs was Asshur-bani-pal, who died in 626. Even the later years of his reign seem to have witnessed the beginning of the decline, and after him there arose none who could hold the ramshackle empire together. Babylon, the greatest of the subject states, revolted under the stress of the new vigour infused into her by the Chaldean dynasty which rose to power in the South. In combination with the Aryan races of the eastern mountains, she made a determined attack on the common enemy, and in 612 succeeded in taking and destroying Nineveh herself. In the meantime, Egypt, which had also passed through a time of domestic confusion, found new life under Ethiopian leadership. The young king, Necho, came to Assyria's help, and from 616 onwards led a yearly expedition into Mesopotamia. The fall of Nineveh did not end the struggle, and in 608, as he moved eastward, Necho put Josiah to death. Three months later, probably on his way back to Egypt, he settled the affairs of Judah. Three more years of warfare followed, ending in the final overthrow of the Egyptian forces at Carchemish on the Euphrates in 605. Never again was Egypt to claim the hegemony of civilisation.

It was inevitable that Judah should be affected by what was happening on the larger stage. As in other cases—e.g., that of Rome—the breaking up of the great Assyrian empire weakened the barriers which had kept out the wild tribes of the north and east. The mixed hordes known to the Greek as Scythians made a series of inroads into western Asia which seem to have continued with greater or less force for about a quarter of a century. Their aim was possibly Egypt, and it seems probable (though the statement is sometimes disputed) that their first raids carried them over Palestine. It is, indeed, difficult to see how that country could have escaped if there were any real invasion from the north at all It is hardly to be supposed that their forces in any way resembled an organised army Miscellaneous and heterogeneous bands of people, collected by the hope of plunder and following no single leader, poured one after another over western Asia during this period. From time to time, it is true, these bands would unite into larger bodies which could meet and even defeat the armies of the more settled peoples in the open field, but there seems to be no instance on record of their having prosecuted a successful siege of any duration. Our information is vague and uncertain, and dates are hardly to be assigned with any accuracy. But it seems clear that they threatened Egypt at some point in the last quarter of the seventh century, and that they played a part in the fortunes of the Philistine cities in this period. The only direct evidence for their attacks on Judah itself is to be found in the references made by Zephaniah and Jeremiah to an enemy from the North. It is difficult to see what other enemy could have threatened Judah at this time, and the description given of the invaders is not unsuitable to the Scythians.

It seems clear, then, that Judah was ravaged, and that for a time there was something approaching a panic in the country. But Jerusalem was never seriously assaulted, and the storm passed. Historical interest turns to the internal affairs of the nation. In 621 the young king, Josiah, inaugurated a religious revival which began with the restoration of the Temple buildings, which had fallen into disrepair. During the progress of the work a Law-book was discovered, which is clearly to be identified with Deuteronomy or a part thereof. The novel element in this book was the insistence on the concentration of worship at a single sanctuary, and the abolition of the local shrines where the old syncretistic worship was still carried on. The date of the composition of this book is uncertain. It claims to be an account of the farewell speeches of Moses —at least in the form which the book now has—but it is probable that it had not long been written when it was discovered. It is obviously an attempt to secure by some sort of compromise the nobler conception of religion for which the eighth century Prophets had stood. Sacrifice could still be offered, but must be confined to circles where the whole could be overseen, regulated, and freed from the abuses which had marked the cults of the "high places." Subsidiary adjustments in the ordinary life of the people were also made. The flesh of domestic animals was secularised, and might be eaten apart from sacrifice. For the three great festivals, all males must come to the central sanctuary. The old altars had formed a refuge for persons who had reason to fear arrest or execution, and this function was in future to be fulfilled by " cities of refuge." The priests of the old local shrines were to take up their residence in Jerusalem itself, and to share in whatever dues were paid by the faithful. At the same time special care was taken to recommend them to the charity of their neighbours.

Josiah proceeded to carry into effect the provisions of this newly found Law-book. Messengers were sent throughout the whole country, and the first application of its principles was at the Passover of 620, when men noted that in all the history of the monarchy there had been no such celebration. Other reforms also took place. The land was cleared of all the illicit cults which had become familiar during the last century, whether they were those of the king or of the people. It is noticeable that special attention is called to the fact that the royal house of Judah itself had not been guiltless, and that Josiah made as clean a sweep of the apostasies of the palace as of those of the country at large. None could charge him with having laid burdens on his people which he was not prepared to bear himself.

It would seem that the prophetic religion had now established itself for a time. But it failed to get a real grip of the national character and spirit. It secured the externals of the purer faith, but did not—perhaps could not—secure that higher spirituality for which Hosea had pleaded. It may be possible to make people sober by Act of Parliament, but it is not possible to convert them by such means. The Deuteronomic regime seems to have been maintained only for a dozen years or so. When Necho, in 608, made his northward move, Josiah went to meet him. It is not clear what happened. The Book of Chronicles[1] gives an account of a fierce battle, in which the Jewish king was killed by archers. The Book of Kings[2], on the other hand, has no mention of any battle, but simply states that when Necho saw Josiah, he put him to death. Left with this account alone, the reader would never think of war, but rather of assassination or of judicial execution[3]. Possibly Necho felt that he had reason to distrust the loyalty of his vassal. and needed to have a nominee of his own on the throne of Jerusalem. It was imperative to an Egyptian king that on a northern expedition he should have nothing to fear from the hill state in his rear.

But, whatever the details were, Josiah died, and was succeeded by his second son, Jehoahaz. This was the choice of the people, and suggests that the new monarch was likely to continue his father's tradition. For Josiah had certainly been a popular sovereign, in spite of his iconoclasm. A continuance of the late king's policy was not what Egypt desired, and within a few months Necho had visited Jerusalem, deposed Jehoahaz, sent him down to Egypt in chains, and placed his elder brother on the throne. Perhaps as a concession to nationalist feeling, he changed his nominee's name from Eliakim to Jehoiakim.

The new king was as strong a contrast to his father as a man could well have been. Where Josiah had been a follower of the prophetic view of religion, Jehoiakim at least permitted a return to the old syncretism. Josiah had been thoroughly democratic in conduct and in spirit. He had eaten and drunk with his people, and had made no space about the throne. He had aimed at justice and righteousness in his general administration, and this, even more than his reforming zeal, had endeared him to his people.

[1] II Chron. xxxv. 20-24.   [2] II Ki. xxiii. 29.
[3] I have to thank Canon R. H. Kennett for calling my attention to the difference between these two accounts. On the other hand Herodotus' reference to an Egyptian victory over the Syrians (II. 159) tends to support the account in Chronicles.

Jehoiakim was the oriental Sultan, extravagant, ostenta-
tious, luxurious, with little or no regard for the rights of
personality. To Josiah his subjects had been " brethren " ;
to Jehoiakim they were " slaves." Further, the glimpses
of light we have of him show him to have been the typically
strong but wicked oriental despot. He is the only king of
Judah of whom it is recorded that he dared to put to death
an accredited prophet of Yahweh. Even Jeroboam II. had
not ventured to proceed to such lengths, and the only
other references to such sacrilegious murder are connected
with Ahab, or rather with his foreign wife, Jezebel.

The battle of Carchemish must have gone far to break
up the Egyptian empire, but the exact relations of Jehoiakim
to the contending parties are far from clear. On the whole
it seems that with characteristic strength—for his sins were
never those of the weak man—he tended to remain faithful
to the Egyptian alliance. He did acknowledge allegiance to
Nebuchadrezzar, but failed to maintain it for more than a
few years, and in 597 a Babylonian army was in Judah.
Jerusalem was besieged, but, either before the investment
or early in its course, Jehoiakim died—the only one of the
last six kings of Judah to meet a comparatively peaceful
end. He was succeeded by his young son, Jehoiachin, who,
after a three months' siege, surrendered to the Chaldeans
and was carried off to Babylon, together with the best of
the people and the nobles. In his place a third son of Josiah
was set on the throne, Zedekiah (originally Mattaniah) by
name. Again the historian notes a complete difference in
character. Zedekiah was not wholly a bad man, but he was
essentially weak. He fell an easy prey to Egyptian intrigue,
and after an escape in 592, when it is possible that he was
actually summoned to Babylon, he finally revolted. Again
a Chaldean army besieged Jerusalem. This time there was
no surrender. The city was taken by storm in 586, Zedekiah
attempted to escape, but was captured and brought before
Nebuchadrezzar. His sons were killed before his eyes, and

he himself was blinded and carried off to Babylon.
Jerusalem was left a heap of blackened ruins, and only a
handful of peasants remained to till the soil. From that
time onwards, except for a brief period under the
Maccabees, the Jewish people have never enjoyed a
national and independent government.

It was, however, no part of Nebuchadrezzar's policy to
leave his conquered territories an absolute desert, nor does
he ever seem to have been unnecessarily cruel as judged by
the standards of his time. He appointed as governor,
Gedaliah, a scion of the princely house of Shaphan, and
established the seat of government at Mizpah. For a time
it seemed as if there was a chance for Judah to recover, but
the jealousy of the Ammonites, working through a member
of the old royal family, procured his assassination. The
last remnant of a governing class fled to Egypt, and there
in process of time disappeared. So ended the Israelite
monarchy ; Jerusalem was as Samaria.

The work of four of our canonical prophets is to be
assigned to this period. The activity of Jeremiah covers
practically the whole of it, since his call came in the year
626, and he is last heard condemning his fellow-countrymen
(and women) for apostasy in Egypt after the final flight
thither. He is emphatically the prophet of this period,
and, in a large measure, the source of information as to
the events and their character. Three others seem to have
done their work at separate points in the lifetime of
Jeremiah. The first of these is Zephaniah, whose extant
oracles are probably to be dated about the year 626 ; the
second is Nahum, *circa* 613 ; and the third is Habakkuk,
who appears about the same time as Nahum, though he
deals with very different matters.

Zephaniah is sometimes supposed to have been connected
with the royal house. His genealogy is traced back a good
deal further than that of most prophets, and the line
extends to a certain Hezekiah, who may well have been

the son and successor of Ahaz. The book in which his
oracles have been preserved contains three groups of prophetic matter. The first is concerned with Israel, or rather
with Judah, and ends with ii. 3. (It may be remarked that
most editors regard this verse as a " later interpolation."
Though it has the appearance of coming from a later time
than Zephaniah, it is better to regard it as a conclusion
attached to this little oracular pamphlet. It is significant
in this connection that it comes at the point where a totally
different type of subject is about to be introduced.) The
second oracular group is concerned with non-Israelite
peoples, and goes down to the end of ch. ii. Modern commentators doubt whether the compiler who brought these
oracles together was right in attributing vv. 8-11 (oracles
against Moab and Ammon) to Zephaniah himself. The third
group consists of a single oracle in iii. 1-5. To this have
been attached a couple of isolated floating verses (which of
course may have been Zephaniah's) and a group of
oracles predicting a happy spiritual and material future
for Israel. This is just the type of conclusion that compilers
loved to append to their collections, and modern students
agree that Zephaniah himself had no hand in them.

What has thus survived from this prophet contains
little that can be called a real contribution to the religious
thinking of the people or of the race. In the main, what
Zephaniah had to say had already been said by Amos,
Hosea, and Micah, particularly the first. There are details,
of course, in which a somewhat different situation is
reflected. The various forms which the apostasy of the
people took are characteristic of Jerusalem, and of the
Jerusalem of the seventh century. It is interesting to find
that they bear some resemblance to those forms of illicit
cultus which Josiah removed (showing incidentally that
these oracles belong to the pre-Deuteronomic period).
Such is the worship of the heavenly bodies on the roofs,

[1] Cf. i. 5.

whilst the mention of the Ammonite god suggests the traditions of the reign of Manasseh. " Those who leap over the threshold "[1] may be adherents of some Philistine cult,[2] and the deeper meaning of apostasy is brought out in the case of those who decline to believe that Yahweh will take any action at all—in other words, that He is helpless and negligible.[3]

Like his predecessors, Zephaniah noted and condemned the social iniquity of his age and home. It is the theme of the longest continuous passage in the book—iii. 1-5—and it is noticeable, especially if the current view of his pedigree be right, that it is the sins of the governing classes that are especially denounced. Princes, judges, prophets, priests— all alike are faithless to their true vocation and function. It is the business of the princes to protect people—instead, they use their strength to pounce on and destroy men. It is the duty of the judges to assign property to its rightful owner—instead they cling to their causes till they have appropriated in bribes or fees all that is in question. It is the task of the Prophets to assure themselves that the oracles which they deliver are the genuine word of Yahweh —instead, they recklessly pour out unauthenticated " oracles " which can only deceive men. It is the work of the priests to distinguish between the holy and the profane, and to see that the true Divine instruction is given to the worshipper—instead, they have confused all religious distinctions and criminally distorted the revelation of Yahweh. And all this has its due punishment. Yahweh is in the midst of the city. He is perfect in everything in which the leaders of Israel are lacking, His vengeance on the criminals is not described, but there is a sense of awe produced by this reticence which is even more effective than elaborate threats.

In one important point Zephaniah does take up and advance upon the views of Amos. This is in his picture of

[1] *Cf.* i. 9. [2] *Cf.* I. Sam. v. 5. [3] *Cf.* i. 12.

the Day of Yahweh. Amos had been content to mention it
in rather vague terms as a day of calamity and not of
prosperity, and of darkness rather than light. It is true
that he adds one of his most powerful similes, but this is
still a simile. Zephaniah has allowed the picture to grow
in clearness and in definition. He sees it as a festival of
Yahweh.   Guests have been invited, and the whole is
regarded as a great sacrifice. It is true that the addition to
the earlier idea—or to the earlier expression of the idea—
is only of the slightest, but it does mark the fact that in
people's minds the conception of the Day of Yahweh was
growing, and was developing towards a recognisable system
of eschatology. It was eschatology which ultimately
succeeded prophecy in the thought of Israel, but its roots
are as old as those of prophecy itself, if not older.[1]

Like Amos, Zephaniah had something to say about other
nations than Israel. But there is one notable difference.
Amos tells of ruin which will befall the people of whom he
speaks because of wrong that they have done. Zephaniah
has not one word of denunciation of sin or crime on the
part of the foreign sufferers, even on Nineveh, for ii. 15
is almost certainly a compiler's conclusion to the section,
being partly taken from Is. xlvi. 8. The difference is
significant, for in Zephaniah Yahweh is a God who is
omnipotent in dealing with other peoples, in Amos he
is also the universal Lord of morality, and whoever in the
whole wide world offends against His conscience will have
to account to Him.

The general impression, then, which the reader obtains
from the Book of Zephaniah is that the Prophet is a
reflection of Amos.   He has little to add to the
thought of his great predecessor, and does not help Israel
towards a fuller light on the things of God. But he does
interpret events which are taking place around him in the

[1] See Ch. XIV.

light of the truths grasped and stated by the earlier prophets and thus stands in the genuine line of tradition.

In Nahum we have a Prophet who presents almost as complete a contrast as possible to Zephaniah. In fact, it may almost be said that he is unique among the Prophets of the Old Testament. The book, as it has come down to us, is a collection of oracular matter, to which an alphabetic poem has been prefixed. It is true that the poem is now incomplete, and even so far as it goes has been subject to a good deal of textual corruption. Various attempts have been made to restore it, and whilst a number of these are interesting and scholarly, none of them carries any real conviction.[1] We must be content to recognise that a large part of the poem has gone beyond recall. It contains a statement of the principle that Yahweh will take vengeance upon His enemies. It would seem that it was prefixed to the oracles of Nahum—with which it has no further connection—because that Prophet's surviving utterances deal largely with Yahweh's vengeance on a particular enemy. It is true that there are hints of relief for Judah, found in i. 12, 13 ; ii. 1, 3 ; but in the main the depths of this feeling must be gathered from the exultant tone of the rest.

The enemy is Nineveh, and her fall is described in vivid and powerful language. One sees the besiegers gather for the assault, the blood-stained shield, the noise and varied tumult of the struggle. The horrors of investment and storm are all there—the scanty water, the blazing fire, the cumbersome heaps of slain. Finally the captivity and enslavement of the survivors, mainly women, whose unspeakable degradation is set before the reader with the lurid brutality of the ancient East.

It is perhaps this descriptive power and wealth of language and metaphor which has been responsible for the preservation of the Prophet's words. For he does not in any sense

---

[1] This is especially true of reconstructions which try to find room for the whole Hebrew alphabet. Those which recognise that it cannot be followed beyond *Samekh* are more successful.

stand in the line of prophetic tradition. The only sins which he condemns are those of Nineveh, and these are denounced, not because they are violations of universal moral laws—Nahum can exult freely over similar cruelties perpetrated on the enemies of Israel—but because it is his own people which has been the victim. In other words, Nahum is a representative of that purely patriotic[1] type of prophecy which has left little trace elsewhere in our Old Testament. Yet in his own day he was probably the more familiar kind of Prophet. It must never be forgotten that the Ecstatic was a very common phenomenon in Jerusalem, and that the tone and views of our canonical Prophets were rather the exception. It was all very well for later ages to dub men "false Prophets," but their own day had little opportunity of deciding between the two classes. There is no reason to doubt that Nahum and those like him honestly believed that they had the direct commission of Yahweh, and were really announcing His word to their people. Their defect was one of mind rather than of will. It was possible for others to deduce the true character of Yahweh ; it was possible for them also. Yet they failed, and in their failure left a warning for all succeeding generations. They may have been popular in their own day, and won the approval of the great crowd. But even consensus is not an infallible test of truth, and in the long run it was the lonely men, Zephaniah and Jeremiah and their like, who led their people and ultimately the world forward to a growing appreciation of the one living and true God. What Jeremiah would have said about Nahum is beyond dispute ; he was almost certainly amongst those prophets whom the latter denounced, and we cannot be too grateful for the preservation of his oracles, in that they show us one at least of the dangers from which the world has been delivered.

[1] He recognises atrocities committed on other nations, but one may doubt if he would have done so had Israel not been involved.

The birth-place and origin of Nahum are a matter of uncertainty. He is called an " Elkoshite," but where Elkosh was no one knows. The vividness with which he describes the last scenes of Nineveh has led some students to believe that his home was actually in Assyria. But that seems unlikely, and archæological research may at any time throw more light on the place with which he is associated.

Still less is known about Habakkuk. No genealogy, no home is mentioned, and it is difficult to see how his very name can be connected with any known Hebrew root. Yet, in spite of this obscurity, he holds a most important place in the history of Hebrew thought. The book which bears his name resembles that of Nahum in one respect. It is a collection of oracles to which a poem has been added, a poem which seems to have had no original connection either with the Prophet or with his utterances. This is ch. iii. Chs. i. and ii. begin with oracular matter which seems to be fairly homogeneous down to ii. 5. This was probably the earliest booklet of oracles, and there has been attached to it a series of five denunciations of various sorts of wrong-doing. These were probably all " floating oracles," collected by a compiler ; the last of them, ii. 18-20, is almost certainly post-exilic, and another, ii. 12-14, is simply a cento of phrases from other writings. In considering the Prophet Habakkuk they may all be neglected.

The actual reference of what remains has been a matter of some dispute. I. 1-4 describe the oppression of the wicked, and ask for vengeance. Apparently the criminals are Jews. Verses 5-11 give a vigorous description of the coming vengeance which will be wrought by the hands of the Chaldeans. The rest, i. 11—ii. 5, contains a larger question and the answer which the Prophet received.[1] The prosperity of certain sinners is involved, and it is held that these are the Chaldeans themselves—both executioners and criminals.

---

[1] It should be remarked that some modern students regard this section as being much later than the time of Habakkuk.

It seems more likely that the oppressors are the Egyptians, or Jehoiakim, whom they placed on the throne for their own purposes. In that case the question of i. 13 may have some reference to the fate of Josiah, or even Jehoahaz. The difficulties have been enhanced for commentators by their assumption that the whole, i. 2—ii. 5, is intended to be a continuous passage. This is, of course, unnecessary, and the references in i. 11—ii. 5 may have nothing whatever to do with those in i. 2-10.

Much of what the Prophet has to say is familiar, especially in i. 2-10. Oppression by the Jewish noble or by the foreigner was all too frequent an occurrence in ancient Jerusalem. And even the language contains more than one reminiscence of Jeremiah. Nor is the idea novel that Yahweh will punish even His own people Israel if they fail to observe His moral law. To Amos and his great successors the fact that Israel was a people of special privilege meant that special responsibility rested on them, and that failure therein would spell disaster. To them, Yahweh was Lord, not merely of creation and of history, but of universal morality. Here, at least, Habakkuk had nothing to add.

Nevertheless, as far as our knowledge goes, he was the first to see one of the most important deductions man has ever made from that doctrine of the morality of God. This is contained in the question of i. 12a, 13, a question which man has never yet wholly answered, and perhaps never will :[1]

> " Art thou not from of old,
>   O Yahweh, my holy God,
> Too pure of eyes to see ill,
>   Nor on trouble canst thou gaze ?
> Why then silently gaze upon traitors,
>   When the wicked engulfeth the righteous ? "

---

[1] 12b seems to be a marginal note which has been copied into the text by mistake.

" Seeing " in the East means more than it does in the West. It frequently implies seeing with satisfaction. Where the West says " I cannot bear him," the East says " I cannot see him." The argument then is, " Thou, O Yahweh, art too pure to endure any kind of suffering "— the Hebrew word for " ill " has not necessarily any suggestion of moral evil, and the word for " trouble " may mean simply exhausting toil—" then how is it that thou canst acquiesce in the existence of suffering, endure the moral iniquity of suffering inflicted by the wicked on the righteous ? " To this day men are still asking this question, and still fail to find a complete answer.

Two points arise at once. One is that such a question could have been asked nowhere except in Israel, and under no conditions except under the influence of the prophetic teaching as to the moral character of God. A distribution of happiness and woe which is not based on merit is always an awkward fact from the practical point of view, but it does not become a religious problem till one believes in a God with a sense of justice. During the Great War, all Christians, pacifist and militarist alike, felt that God's permission of war was a problem. It could not be a problem in the same sense to a Hindu who included the goddess Kali in his Pantheon, nor to the Moslem who held that in certain circumstances war might, in the form of a Jihad, be a duty and even a sacrament. To us, brought up in an atmosphere which has been steadily (albeit very slowly) growing more Christian for centuries, the righteousness of God is a truism ; to every race and faith except the Jew and the Christian it has been and is a paradox. It was only on the basis of such teaching as Amos gave to his people that such a question as Habakkuk's could have been asked.

The second point is that, given such teaching as to the character of Yahweh, the question was inevitable. It is true that men are slow to realise the implications of their own beliefs, especially when those beliefs are new, but in the long run they will be discerned. Sooner or later the problem is bound to arise, and to demand an answer of some kind. Generation after generation of Jew and Christian has sought to find a solution, and from time to time new light has appeared, but it must be freely granted that man has not yet succeeded. It may be that under the limitations of time and space he never will, or again it may be that some day he will see, in spite of his limitations, with clarity and certainty the reasons for this undeniable inequality in the apportionment of suffering and joy. One thing is beyond doubt. No problem has contributed more to man's thinking about God or to his study of God's ways, and if the final solution ever is found, it will of itself open out into more problems such as have never as yet entered into the heart of man. That is the way God works in His self-revelation ; each step attained is but the starting point for fresh progress.

Habakkuk does not attempt to solve his own question by a process of reasoning. Such a course is wholly foreign to the Hebrew genius, and the most thorough and daring enquiry into this matter they produced—that of the Book of Job—fails utterly to offer a philosophical explanation. Rather it is intuition which will give to such a mind what it seeks. God must Himself offer the revelation ; man's share is to ask and to place himself in an attitude of receptivity. This Habakkuk does, and receives the famous reply, " The righteous shall live by his faithfulness." The meaning is obscure, but it seems most likely that the Prophet intended to imply that fidelity to God was in itself the truest reward, and that apart from this no external prosperity or immunity from pain was worth anything whatsoever. This is an interesting and valuable comment on the problem rather than a solution.

It would be tempting to follow the later history of Hebrew thought on this question, but it would demand too lengthy a treatment. Suffice it to say that its ripest fruit in Jewish thought did not appear till some centuries after prophecy had ceased to be a living force in the religion of the nation. In the Book of Job, and later still in the terrible sufferings of the Maccabean times, it led the Jew to realise that there is no solution in this life, and that therefore a solution must be sought after death. In other words, Jewish religion deduced its ultimate doctrine of immortality from the very nature and character of God, as the righteous ruler of the universe. And this truly colossal achievement of the human spirit is ultimately based on Habakkuk's question.

X

JEREMIAH

THERE are certain great periods of transition in human history which mark as it were the fluid passages between longer stretches of comparatively stable conditions. Not the least important of these was the last quarter of the seventh century B.C. Old landmarks disappeared, a new adjustment of the nations came into being. As we have seen, the storm period opened with the inroads of the wild northern hordes. There followed the final collapse of Nineveh, for several centuries the supreme power in the civilised world ; then the fatal defeat of Egypt, who was never again to raise her head as a first rank world power. For a brief but brilliant century Babylon became the queen of the nearer East, till she in turn fell before the rising power of Persia. Yet even that change, though it introduced an era of greater stability, was a less profound upheaval than that which preceded it between the years 625 and 600.

Such a time must have had its great men—indeed we know it had. Nebuchadrezzar is one of the outstanding figures of history. Others would probably have attained to fame in any other age. Necho of Egypt was no ordinary man. The agents and subordinates of the Babylonian king cannot have been weaklings ; kings like Nebuchadrezzar know how to choose their officials. Yet of them all there is none whose name has been handed down to us with special emphasis—except perhaps Nebuchadrezzar himself. All have vanished, and it is much if the average man of to-day has but heard once or twice in his life the names of such men as Nebuzaradan, the actual conqueror of Jerusalem. One man has survived, and only one, as a real and living personality, whose influence is not dead, and who has a meaning for us to-day no less than for his own time. This was one who came from one of the smallest of the states involved in the great cosmic upheaval. Even amongst his own people he was without honour or respect, and made little if any impression upon his contemporaries. Yet it is not Necho or Nebuzaradan or even Nebuchadrezzar himself whose name and personality live to-day, it is Jeremiah of Anathoth.

The date of his birth is uncertain, but it must have been somewhere between 650 and 640 B.C. He belonged to the priestly family of Anathoth, a small village some few miles to the north of Jerusalem. His relatives must have been the guardians and attendants of the shrine, the " high place " of the village, and this fact needs to be borne in mind throughout if we would understand his life and his message. His first ecstatic experiences seem to have coincided with the Scythian inroads, and to have been concerned with them. This took place in the year 626, and it is five years before we hear of him again. Then the Law was discovered. Jeremiah seems to have steeped himself in the thought of the eighth century Prophets, especially of Hosea, and appears to have welcomed the Deuteronomic reform as giving some opportunity for the realisation of the true prophetic ideals.[1] He threw himself

---

[1] This has been disputed, but the discussion turns mainly on the historicity of ch. xi., and there is a growing tendency to accept the substantial accuracy of the narrative contained therein.

into the movement, and became one of the preachers of
the new law. It was inevitable that this should bring him
into conflict with his own family, and he had to bear the
sorrow of knowing that those whom he loved best were
prepared even to take his life, though in view of the fact
that he represented the royal party, it is probable that
they did not contemplate actual violence till after the
tragedy of Megiddo in 608. It was possibly this which drove
him from his home. Jehoiakim was in no sense sympathetic
towards his father's policy, and the reaction which set in
on his accession once more brought Jeremiah to the front
as an apostle of righteousness and purity in worship.
Entering the Temple on a great festival, when he was sure
of a large audience, he gave utterance to an oracle which
has been preserved in a revised form in ch. vii. There stood
with him another Prophet, Uriah by name. The audacious
conduct of these two men came to Jehoiakim's ears, and he
took measures for their arrest. Uriah lost his nerve and
fled to Egypt. His extradition was easily arranged
—Jehoiakim was a vassal of the Egyptian throne—and he
was brought back and put to death. Jeremiah escaped
by simply concealing himself.[1] He remained in hiding till
after the battle of Carchemish, whose general importance
he seems to have realised to the full. For some reason
which has never been ascertained he was unable to appear
in public, so took a step which, as far as we know, was
entirely novel for a Prophet, but ultimately had a far-
reaching influence on the character of Jewish religion. He
secured the services of a professional writer, and dictated
to him a collection of the oracles which had been uttered by
him up to date. Baruch, the writer in question, took the
completed volume and read it publicly in the Temple.
He was heard by a number of the more prominent nobles,
who felt that this was a matter which must be reported

[1] The circumstances are described in ch. xxvi.

to Jehoiakim at once. But they seem to have had no ill will against either Jeremiah or Baruch, and gave the friendly advice that it was better for both to remain in concealment. They then took the volume to the king, and read it in his presence. Before they had proceeded far he took the matter into his own hands and destroyed the book in the dramatic fashion which is so familiar to every reader. Doubtless he thought to put an end to a movement which might be used for political purposes. But the word of Yahweh was not so to be escaped, and Jeremiah dictated the contents of another roll.[1]

Two symbolic actions ascribed to Jeremiah may have been performed in the later years of Jehoiakim's reign. One is the purchase and spoiling of a linen girdle,[2] the other the emptying and breaking of a bottle.[3] The result of this latter incident was a conflict with the civil authorities. We have no data as to the prophet's activity or fortunes during the siege of 597-596, but the account is fuller for the reign of Zedekiah than for any other period in his life. He held strong views as to the difference between the older nobility who had been carried away with Jehoiachin and those who were left, and gave expression to these views in the Vision of the Figs.[4] To the same period belongs (apparently) the symbolical action of the making and wearing of the yoke,[5] which brought Jeremiah into conflict with Hananiah.[6] It would seem that at this time there was already a movement which aimed at the overthrow of Babylon and the liberation of the exiles. One may conjecture that popular prophecy, represented both in Jerusalem and in Babylon, had a strongly apocalyptic tone, and that men had been led by it to expect some miraculous interference in the order of things. Certainly there was a strong hope of an immediate return—a hope to which Jeremiah could lend no support—and a direct personal

---

[1] See ch. xxxvi. [2] xiii. 1-11. [3] xix. 1-18. [4] Ch. xxiv
[5] Ch. xxvii. [6] Ch. xxviii.

attack was made upon him. A letter was sent from Babylon
to the chief of the Temple police, asking that he might be
silenced. Of the details we have no record, but the attempt
failed, and Jeremiah took the opportunity of an embassy
going from Jerusalem to Babylon to send a strong denunciation of his enemies there.[1] The story reaches its fullest
detail during the final attack on Jerusalem. Jeremiah
could see only one issue to the struggle, and never ceased
to warn his fellow countrymen that their only hope of
individual safety lay in desertion to the Chaldeans. The
siege began, and though a demonstration was made by
Egypt which forced the Chaldeans for a time to raise it,
the Prophet insisted that the relief was only temporary.[2]
In the meantime some question of the family property
in Anathoth demanded his presence in his native village.
He was arrested at the gate of the city as he went out,
accused of desertion to the enemy—not an unnatural
charge in view of the message he had been giving—and
thrown into prison. There he was consulted by Zedekiah,
and secured some alleviation. The family business remained
unsettled till one of his relatives came into Jerusalem, and
Jeremiah took the opportunity of exhibiting his faith that
in spite of the impending calamity there would one day be
a restoration, for he had the deeds of the property carefully
made out and preserved.[3] At the same time he continued
his prediction of the immediate doom of the city, and the
nobles felt that this was a piece of dangerous " defeatism "
which must be stopped. Accordingly they took measures
to remove him. His prophetic character probably made it
impossible for them to proceed to actual murder, so they
secured the royal permission—given with pathetic helplessness—to lower him into a disused well, which was thick
with mud. (It must be remembered that the mention of
the mud means that it was at least waist deep, for nothing

[1] Ch. xxix.   [2] xxxvii. 1-10.   [3] Ch. xxxii.

much shallower is thought worth particular mention in an eastern city !) There he was left to starve. But the intercession of an Ethiopian eunuch, Ebedmelech, saved him, and he was with difficulty drawn to the surface and returned to his old prison. Again and again Zedekiah consulted him, always receiving the one answer, " Surrender and you will be safe ; maintain the resistance and you will be ruined." But the weak king could not make up his mind to the final step, and at length the end came.

For forty years Jeremiah had lived daily through the last agonies of the fall of Jerusalem. But now the blow had fallen, and the result to him seems to have been a great sense of relief. He was kindly treated by the Chaldeans, and allowed to settle with Gedaliah at Mizpah. It appears that here for the first time a gleam of hope shot across his sad horizon. It was possible that under this new leader— brave, kindly, pious, chivalrous—the restoration of Judah might begin. To this time, then, belong the brighter oracles included in chs. xxx. and xxxi. But, if we are right in supposing that Jeremiah at last found light, the interval was only a brief one, and a yet darker night fell after the murder of Gedaliah. Jeremiah was consulted as to the best route for the fugitives to take into Egypt. For ten days he had no message to give, and when the oracle did come to him it was not such as Jochanan and his friends sought, for the orders were to stay where they were, since no harm would befall them at the hands of the Chaldeans. But they would not listen, and took Jeremiah with them. His first utterance in Egypt was to proclaim the ultimate subjection of that country to Babylon.

Once again we hear of him in Egypt. The women, with the consent of their menfolk, had taken to the worship of the Queen of Heaven. Jeremiah protested, but in vain. To him it was the real end. It meant that the association between Israel and Yahweh was finally broken, and that they would no more be His people and He would be no more their God. Tradition says that Jeremiah was stoned to death by the Jews in Egypt. Such a close to his life is not impossible, not even improbable. But, for him, the real end came with the last words recorded of him.

The Book of Jeremiah is one of the most interesting and complex of all the prophetic volumes. Like that of Isaiah, it contains a number of smaller oracular collections. But in the case of Jeremiah these oracular collections are far from being the only material which the main compiler had at his disposal. He had at least two other types of matter, both written in prose. In the one case the story is told in the first person; the Prophet speaks himself, and the substance is obviously for the most part oracular matter which has been reduced to prose form in transcription. In the other case the story is told in the third person, and the greater part of the material consists of narratives about the Prophet rather than his actual words. The distinction is not absolute; there is narrative in the first person (as in ch. i.), and there are at least reports or oracular utterances in the third person (as in ch. xxvi.). Sometimes, though rarely, it is possible that the same story is told in both types of writing; perhaps the only obvious case is that of ch. vii. (first person) and ch. xxvi. (third person), where it is clearly the same incident that is described.

We have, then, these three classes of passage, oracular poetry, prose in the first person, and prose in the third person. The compiler's method has been to take each little oracular collection and to prefix to it a section or passage from one or other of the prose portions. The preference has been, at any rate in the earlier part of the book, for sections of the second type, for the third person first occurs in ch. xix. After the whole of the poetic material had been thus employed, there remained a good deal of prose, especially in the third person, and this has been added at the end of the whole collection. Sometimes both types appear as introductory as in the case of ch. xxv., where they are followed in the Hebrew text by a comparatively brief poetic section describing Yahweh's relations with foreign peoples. It should be added that the sections of the third type are usually attributed (with some reason) to Baruch.

Another point of peculiar interest needs to be mentioned. The book seems to have been known and used by the Egyptian Jews at a fairly early period, and they developed a tradition (now represented only in the Greek translation indicated as the LXX) which often diverges widely from that of Palestine as given to us in the Hebrew text. The most striking instance of this is to be seen in a collection of oracles against foreign nations which is found in the Hebrew text after ch. xlv. But in the LXX it occupies an entirely different position, appearing in the middle of the Massoretic ch. xxv., and taking the place of v. 14. A further divergence is to be seen in the fact that the order in which these oracles occur is not the same in the two editions. We have here one of those collections grouped according to subject which are not infrequent in the prophetic books. Some modern students would deny that Jeremiah had anything to do with these at all, and few would assign the whole to this prophet. It is generally agreed, for instance, that the group of oracles against Babylon (chs. l, li., Hebrew text) is not Jeremiah's in any part, except that one of his oracles originally aimed at Judah has been modified to suit Babylon. It evidently maintained an independent existence after being incorporated in ch. vi. Some of the oracles against Moab also appear in Is. xv. and xvi., and some of the matter dealing with Edom has been included in the book of "Obadiah." On the other hand there is something to be said in favour of the Jeremianic authorship of two at least of the oracles against Egypt, and it is probable that the collection originally included also those against Philistia and Damascus. Much of the remainder is of the nature of that

prophetic commonplace which is liable to appear in every
collection of threats against foreign nations. There are
one or two other sections which appear to be real inter-
polations, the most conspicuous of which is x. 1-16. This
section contains the curious Aramaic verse 11—apparently
a spell to use when confronted with the gods of the heathen
—and other matter concerned with the conflict between the
later Judaism and the outside world. It should be added
that the historical appendix in ch. lii. seems to have been
added by the main compiler of the book to round off the
whole, in much the same way as the final compiler of the
Book of Isaiah attached chs. xxxvi.-xxxix. to the end of
his collection.

Mention has already been made of the influence of Hosea
on Jeremiah. Indeed, the two had much in common.
One is struck by the fact that Jeremiah had comparatively
little to add to the theology of the prophetic movement.
He believed as strongly as his predecessors in the profoundly moral character and ethical appeal of Yahweh.
No less than they, he laid stress on the inexorable law that
sin means suffering, sooner or later. One at least of his
metaphors seems to have been taken directly from Hosea.
It is that found especially in iii. 6-18, a passage whose
originality has been challenged, but is practically certified
by the use Ezekiel made of it. To Jeremiah, as to the others,
the only hope of his people lay in their return to Yahweh.
For He had complete control over all human affairs, and
the invader, whether Scythian or Chaldean, was simply
the messenger of His will.

But every reader will admit that the main interest of
this Prophet lies not in his theology and his teaching, but
in his personality. Whatever he looked like to his contemporaries, to us, looking back over the centuries, he
appeals as a singularly lovable man. He was not of the
stuff of which one supposes Prophets to be made. Modest,
tender, shy, nervous, he was interested in the simple things

of the country and of the home. He, more than any other
of whom we know, stood in need of the reiterated promises
of strength and support with which his ministry opened.
The call came to him while he was still young. Otherwise
he would not have had a period of activity of between
forty and fifty years. His own description of himself in
i. 6 does not necessarily refer to age, but rather to standing.
He was a dependent, and had never had to bear the
responsibility of family or official life. From this habit of
subordination he had to take upon himself one of the most
difficult tasks that can be laid upon a man. He had to stand
alone in the face of others, high and low, near and far,
and to say things to them which would be unpleasant
and possibly irritating. The natural shrinking from
publicity which seems to have been characteristic of him
was greatly increased by this, and again and again
he must have had to fall back on the promise that
he should be as a fortified city in the face of enemies.
Like others of his kind, he was fond of his country home and
brought from it much knowledge of and interest in the wild
things. He had watched the flight of the migratory
birds on their annual journeys,[1] and knew the nesting
habits of the partridge.[2] He had listened to the roar of
the leopard and the howl of the jackal, as they prowled
outside the village gate.[3] The reader is struck by a sense
of sympathy with the animals in their distresses and their
sufferings, especially in drought.[4] The farm animals,[5] too,
were familiar to him, as well as the antelope and the wild
ass. But his greatest sympathy was always reserved for
his own kind. He was under no illusions—he had been
taught, perhaps, by introspection—as to the weaknesses
of human nature.[6] It was in no external or censorious
spirit that he denounced their wrongdoing. He loved their

[1] *Cf.* viii. 7.   [2] *Cf.* xvii. 11.
[3] *Cf.* iv. 16, 17 (probably the text should be emended in this sense).
[4] *Cf.* xiv. 5, 6.   [5] *Cf.* ii. 23, 24.   [6] *Cf.* xvii. 9.

company, and it would have been his highest delight to have shared in the simple life of his friends. His inner longing was ever for peace and for the events of a life lived in peace. Few things can have been harder for him than the prohibition of marriage, with its promise of a home and loved wife and children, his exclusion from the peasant revelry of marriage, and from the sympathetic participation in his neighbours' griefs.[1] We gather that little babies appealed to him.

It is necessary to realise all this in order to appreciate the cost of his prophetic service. He was a man thus formed for quietness and sympathy, yet forced to surrender both by a double and overpowering passion. On the one hand he was impelled by a love for his country, on the other by a love for her (and his) God. His dearest wish, his supreme aim, was to see the two united. A part, at least, of the tragedy of his life was due to the awful fact that, from the death of Josiah onwards, at any rate, he was compelled to watch Judah drifting away from her spiritual and political safety towards the brink of that cataract over which she ultimately plunged. His was the unspeakable suffering of knowing and seeing clearly all that was to befall her, of crying to her to take that course which alone could bring her security, and of finding that his warning fell on utterly deaf ears. Yet he never flinched or failed, and faithfully bore his cross to the very end.

Not only in his doctrines but also in his attitude towards politics Jeremiah followed the traditions of Amos and Isaiah. He was not—could not be—blind to the great world movements which were taking place around him. His was a clearer vision than that which was granted to most of his contemporaries, and he seems to have understood as no other man of the day did, the significance of the battle of Carchemish. In all probability it was this

[1] *Cf.* xvi. 1-9.

event alone which called for any comments from him on the neighbouring peoples. He was necessarily interested in the Scythians, because they vitally affected Israel's immediate condition. So also in later years he was concerned with the Chaldeans. But in both these cases the interest is in the Israelite point of view, not in that of the other nation. With the Egyptians,[1] the Philistines,[2] and the Damascenes[3] the case is different. It is their ruin or danger that is in question, not their relations with Judah, and the danger in all these cases seems to have come from Babylon. Jeremiah was no friend to Egypt, and there is a certain tone of triumph in his oracles over her fall. Like other Prophets, he appears to have felt that the great southern power was the evil genius of the Palestinian states, and this feeling can only have been intensified by the tragedy of Josiah's death. But the rest were little more than fellow-victims with Judah herself. The aspect of the world had suddenly changed, and few appreciated the fact as thoroughly as the Prophet of Jerusalem.

In domestic politics Jeremiah played a comparatively small part. He is not represented as having the kind of political influence which we generally associate with Isaiah. When he came into conflict with statesmen and official persons, it was usually as a direct result of his own preaching. Yet he held strong views about the various kings whom he knew. For Josiah he had a sincere respect and possibly affection. Curiously enough, his approval is not based on the religious reforms with which he sympathised, but on the personal character of the king, especially in contrast with his son Jehoiakim. There is a very strong vein of democratic feeling in Jeremiah, and Josiah's freedom from any form of personal pride and his attitude of good fellowship towards his fellow citizens won the hearty approval and esteem of the Prophet.[4]

[1] *Cf.* Ch. xlvi.   [2] *Cf.* Ch. xlvii.   [3] *Cf.* xlix. 23-27.
[4] *Cf.* xxii. 15-16.

Moreover the general principles on which the government of Josiah was conducted were those of uprightness, fairness and honour, which so much appealed to all the Prophets. Josiah—apart altogether from the Deuteronomic reform—came near to being the ideal king.

Of his successor, Jehoahaz, Jeremiah has but little to say,[1] but that little is couched in terms of regret, and we are left with the sense that the deportation of this king was a tragedy for Israel only second to the death of his father. But of all the monarchs under whose reign he lived and worked, it was Jehoiakim who most excited his denunciations. Once again we are conscious of the two motives, one religious and one social. In neither direction was there anything to be said for Jehoiakim. The type of kingship at which he aimed recalled the worst features and abuses of the reign of Solomon. It is possible that the seventh century saw the son and successor of David through other eyes than ours, and was inclined to dwell on features in his policy and government which we are apt to miss. In so far as Jehoiakim may have seen in Solomon an ideal, it was the splendour of the oriental sultan which he admired. Jehoiakim, too, would build magnificent palaces—at the expense of his subjects. Such projects could be carried out only by forced service, hardly to be distinguished from slavery. As always, luxurious ostentation and social iniquity went hand in hand, regal magnificence was to be attained only through sweated labour.[2] From the days of Elijah onwards this had been one of the standing complaints of the Prophets, and in the case of Jehoiakim the evils they had so freely denounced seemed to have reached their high-water mark. We can hardly doubt that it was this, far more than Jeremiah's religious protests, that roused the royal anger and made it impossible for the Prophet to leave his hiding place for the greater part of the reign. Save in the conflict

---

[1] *Cf.* xxii. 10-12.   [2] *Cf.* xxii. 13-19.

between Elijah and Jezebel, we have nowhere so clear an instance of the clash between religion and politics in the history of Israel.

There is a pathos attaching to the name of Jehoiachin which finds an echo in Jeremiah's dirge over him.[1] What he might have been we cannot say, for he never had a chance. Called to the throne at the age of eighteen, he spent the three short months of his reign in a disastrous war, whose issue was not hidden from Jeremiah. Yet the certainty of the doom does not seem to have carried with it a personal condemnation of the king himself. If blame were to be laid anywhere, it fell rather on the young king's mother, Nehushtan. Owing to her position and to her son's youth, she seems to have been the dominant influence in Jewish policy. The slight reference we have to her[2] suggests that she had a fair share of her late husband's outlook and aims, and the new reign seems to have given no sign of improvement. Even if it had been consistent with Jehoiachin's character, there was no time. The first stage of the exile came, and Zedekiah reigned in his nephew's stead.

Allusion has already been made to the character of Zedekiah. What Jeremiah had to meet in the new reign was due not so much to the king's active hostility as to his weakness. Nothing illustrates so clearly the effect of the first deportation as the relations between Jeremiah and the Government. From 607 to 597 he had had to face the royal hostility, and was saved only by the support of the princes, especially by the family of Shaphan.[3] From 596 to 586 he had little or nothing to fear from the malice of the king ; indeed, the respect which Zedekiah felt for him was the only thing which preserved his life from the hatred of the new nobility.[4] Zedekiah himself had not the strength

---

[1] *Cf.* xxii. 24-29.   [2] *Cf.* xiii. 18*ff.*
[3] *Cf.* xxvi. 12-19, xxxvi. 10-12, etc.
[4] These " upstarts " seem to have offered a profound contrast to their predecessors. For Jeremiah's view *cf.* Ch. xxiv.

to maintain an independent policy against the wishes of his court, nevertheless he seems to have felt that Jeremiah was the one person to whom he could turn in his difficulties. Again and again he consulted him, and it was only the inherent vacillation and cowardice of his nature that prevented him from carrying out the Prophet's advice. It may well be that superstition played no small part in determining the attitude of Zedekiah, but it is also possible that he had realised that this man did speak the truth of Yahweh, and that the promises of all the popular and patriotic Prophets were valueless, being no more than the product of their own wishes and desires.

Be that as it may, Zedekiah dared not take the course which Jeremiah recommended to him, and he and his kingdom fell disastrously. Save for brief intervals, such as the height of the Maccabean period, Jewry had had no independent national home for twenty-five centuries. Yet for the moment it did not seem to the Prophet that all was lost. There was still a remnant in the land, and under their leader, Gedaliah, there seemed the possibility that a new life might begin. The Governor was of that same family of Shaphan which had stood faithfully by Jeremiah in earlier days, and though we have no express dirge or lament over his fate, it is clear that there was a very real sympathy in the mind of the Prophet with the head of the new regime. The exact period during which the Mizpah colony maintained its existence is not clear. A superficial reading of the story suggests that it was only a few months, but that is far from being the only possible interpretation of the narrative, and some indications point to a space of three or four years. But whether it were long or short, the evil genius of Judah triumphed once more, and the treacherous assassination of Gedaliah was followed by the cowardly flight into Egypt. There Israel lost the last relics of her national life and faith. The worship of the Queen of Heaven claimed the women, and their men made no protest. Jeremiah, who had foreseen the fall of Egypt, now realised that the last hope was gone. His two great passions, the two interests which it had been his life's work to try to reconcile, were finally shown to be incompatible. With the resignation of despair Jeremiah said, " If you must forsake Yahweh, you must. But this means the utter end of the old covenant. You can be no more His people, and He can be no more your God." Yet even so the Prophet knows that all that really matters is Yahweh. An earlier generation—indeed possibly his own contemporaries—believed that Israel was necessary to Yahweh, that He could not exist as a God apart from His people. This Jeremiah saw to be false. It was Israel who was the dependent partner in the association. Yahweh could do without her, as she could not do without Him. So his last words to the world are : " They shall know whose word shall stand, mine or theirs."[1]

Optimism is sometimes supposed to be the capacity for looking on the bright side of things and ignoring whatever is unpleasant or dangerous. Such is the habit of the traditional ostrich, which is said to bury its head in the sand at the approach of inevitable enemies. But this shallow refusal to face facts is only a travesty of the real thing. Jeremiah had to meet this attitude again and again, and few of his denunciations are more bitter than those launched at men who " healed the broken limbs of the daughter of my people lightly, saying Peace, Peace, where there is no peace."[2] He has been accused of pessimism because he refused to accept this point of view, and because when things were wrong he did not hesitate to say so. Being what he was, and living when he did, how could he have been happy ? Only by giving up the demand for truth and surrendering himself to what he knew to be false could he attain to any sort of peace. This he would not and could not do, for his

[1] xliv. 28.   [2] vi. 14, viii. 11.

was that far truer and more profound optimism which consists in a determined and passionate faith in goodness, which declines to believe that evil, however great it may be, is ever to be chosen in preference to good, and identifies all human success and prosperity with the achievement of that goodness whose starting point and goal alike are to be found in God. No suffering of body, mind or soul, could wring from him an admission of the possibility that good might in the long run fail. It was the basic fact in the universe to him, and in the end it must triumph. Though human stupidity, perversity and selfishness might postpone that end, yet at long last it would be attained —God's word would *stand*. This is the supreme optimism.

Whilst in the maintenance of this conviction and in the expression of this creed Jeremiah had much to face in the way of persecution from people, nobles and kings, he always clung to them. As far as we know, no threat or penalty of man could make him move. He was indeed a " fortified city." But though he steadily held to this grim firmness in his dealings with man, it was otherwise in his relations with his God. It is, indeed, here that Jeremiah has perhaps most to say to the world. For, from the day when he was called, the burden of his ministry lay upon him as a weight almost unbearable. It meant to him the loss of his home, public persecution, the inability to win those social delights which would have made life worth living in itself. This he might have borne, but there was added a deeper and darker suspicion of Yahweh Himself. It must be remembered that men's appreciation of the Divine character—even Jeremiah's—was still in an elementary stage. There can be no doubt that it was believed that Yahweh did from time to time use the very prophetic ecstasy to deceive and trap men to their ruin. There is indeed a word which is practically a technical term for this divine treachery. It is used by Micaiah in his description of the scene in the divine court which was to be fatal to Ahab.[1] Ezekiel even goes as far as to say that such a Prophet might be " enticed " to his own ruin—the willing victim of Divine vindictiveness and deceit.[2] As far as externals went, the true Prophet was not to be distinguished from the false. People therefore needed some clear definition whereby they could know the one from the other. Such a definition was provided by Deuteronomy, which laid it down that the genuineness of a Prophet was to be judged by the fulfilment or otherwise of his words.[3] This, then, was the belief in Jeremiah's day ; his own belief, too. And for years he had prophesied the downfall of his city and the ruin of his people, and it had not come. Men saw in the long-drawn security of the city evidence of the falsity of the Prophet. Jeremiah rebelled more than once against his position. Once he was told that the best thing that could be offered to him was that he should return to his allegiance ; once that he would have to meet difficulties worse than those of which he complained.[5] But all other experiences pale into insignificance beside the awful outburst of xx. 7 ff. For years the word of Jeremiah had failed to come true. People recognised in him the symptoms of the " enticed " Prophet, and with the callous brutality of an early age jeered at him as one trapped and deliberately damned by Yahweh. At last the Prophet had come to believe this of himself. He had struggled to throw off the yoke, but had failed. The fire of prophecy blazed within him, and his whole soul was torn asunder between the impossibility of going on and the impossibility of refraining. Such conflict and agony of spirit have hardly any parallel in the records of man's spiritual life.

With all this it must be remembered that he had no outlook beyond the grave. To ancient Israel, whilst there was no doubt as to the continued existence of man after death—after a fashion—the whole drama, good and evil,

---

[1] *Cf.* I Ki. xxii. 19-23. [2] *Cf.* Ez. xiv. 9.
[3] *Cf.* Dt. xviii. 22. [4] xv. 19 [5] xii. 5.

joy and suffering, the presence or absence of God, must be
played out on the stage of this life. For the dead there
was only Sheol, and the meanest life on earth was preferable
to that. The full heroism of such a man as Jeremiah is
not understood until this is appreciated. For him there
was no martyr crown of glory. For him there was no triumph
in another life. For him there was no prospect of the
solution of doubt and the vanishing of shadows in the fuller
light of God's immediate presence. For him there was no
hope of vindication or compensation in an eternity of
exultant spiritual life. He bore his burden and fought his
fight making every possible sacrifice and with every possible
alleviation reft from him. A life of suffering, of torture,
of loneliness, of despair, lived in the service of a God who
had ruined him and for the sake of a people who persecuted
him—this was to meet with no reward save that sunless
and godless Sheol which was the common lot of righteous
and wicked alike. Yet the effect of this lifelong experience
was to set Jeremiah alone amongst the men of his race.
Later generations saw in him the supreme Prophet, and
rightly. For it was in consequence of this isolation that
he made, though unconsciously, his greatest contribution
to the world's knowledge of God.

It has already been remarked that Jeremiah does not
seem to have added to the theology of Israel any new
doctrine. As far as the formal expression of the nature
and will of God went, he was able only to repeat what his
predecessors had said. But his experience involves an
entirely new conception of the relations between God and
man. In the older view the stress was always laid on the
solidarity of the human group. If we trace back the
story of Israel, we see clearly that people stand in relation
to Yahweh through the tribe, clan, or nation. In
other words the unit of religion on the human side is the
group and not the individual. Achan[1] has to be put to

[1] Josh. vii.

death, not because there is any vindictiveness against him personally, but because he has handled the *tabu*, and through him the contagion has spread to all the people. His execution is a piece of spiritual disinfection, not a punishment. And through all the history of Israel men are treated from the point of view of their relation to the community, in religious matters as in civil. Even the great predecessors of Jeremiah—and Jeremiah himself too—insist that the punishment for individuals' sin falls on the community as a whole. Even in cases where the sin seems to be most personal, as in David's numbering of the people, it is the nation on whom the avenging stroke falls. There are exceptions, but they are very rare, and the general rule is that man does not stand alone in his dealings with Yahweh, but carries with him the whole burden of the human group to which he belongs.

No doubt there is much truth in this, and a fuller recognition of it would save many people from serious worry over problems connected with the indiscriminate apportionment of human suffering. But this cannot to-day be allowed to obscure the other side of the truth, namely, the fact that man does also stand in a very real sense alone with his God. The sinner who cries out " Against thee and thee only have I sinned " stands on a very different level from the men of the older view. And, as far as we know, it was Jeremiah, taught by his own bitter experience, who first of all Israelites realised that he held an immediate personal relation to Yahweh, which was independent of the nation to which he belonged. Hence it is to him, first of all men, that we owe the great utterance which condemns the doctrine—" The fathers have eaten sour grapes and the children's teeth are set on edge."[1] The solidarity of the race may be true, but it is only half the truth, and the full meaning of the religious experience is grasped only when the two halves are admitted. Heredity

[1] xxxi. 29-30.

and environment—to use the more modern terms—account for much, but they will not account for everything. There is such a thing as individual responsibility. Each separate and independent human personality must stand face to face with his God, by and for himself. Personal religion becomes an established reality with Jeremiah.

It is impossible to exaggerate the wealth of the harvest that man has reaped from this lonely seed, sown in agony of tears and blood. From it sprang much of that richness of spiritual life and experience which has made the Psalter the comfort and inspiration of later ages. Without it the characteristic features of the later Judaism would have been impossible. It struck the keynote of the teaching of Jesus about the Fatherhood of God and His care for each of His children. It underlay the evangelical message of the Apostles and of the early Church. It was the fundamental assumption of the great call of the Reformation for repentance and a personal approach to God. Without it there could be no genuine doctrine of a future life, and it is this which has inspired the mysticism inherent in all really efficient Christianity. In a very true and profound sense, Jeremiah was the father of all the saints.

Of this, however, the Prophet himself does not seem to have been wholly conscious. And whilst there was, strictly speaking, no new doctrine which Jeremiah had to offer the world, there was an idea, a phrase, which endured. This was his conception of the New Covenant. In his day, religion was conceived and interpreted in covenant terms. It was in this light that Deuteronomy had appealed to the men who discovered it, and it was under this guise that the new law had attracted the enthusiasm of the young Prophet.[1] As time went on he learnt that a written law could not do all that man needed. Possibly even in the later days of Josiah its weakness had become apparent, and Jeremiah found that

---

[1] *Cf.* ch. xi. though, as remarked above, Jeremiah's approval of Deuteronomy is disputed.

a document was always exposed to the tampering of the scribes.[1] With the reaction under the sons of Josiah the failure of Deuteronomy became more apparent still, and no small part of the sorrow of the Prophet must have lain in the dashing of his early hopes to the ground. He had longed so passionately for a valid union between Yahweh and His people, and this, which had at first promised so much, had now failed utterly. But Yahweh could not fail, and later—it would seem after the destruction of Jerusalem—he gave utterance to the words which have been preserved for us in xxxi. 31-34. The old covenant had been shattered, but a new one would be offered in its place. And this time the weakness of the old would be avoided. It had failed, as Jeremiah saw, because it had been an external thing, written down in a book, and imposed on men by royal or ecclesiastical authority. Not so can the dealings of man with God be rightly ordered. The only authority which is valid in the last resort is that which comes from within. The only covenant which can carry its own fulfilment is that which has a man's personality behind it, which grips his very soul and carries him forward by its own momentum. There is no alteration in the terms, "I will become their God and they shall become my people." But the method of its establishment is to be changed. Deuteronomy, with all its magnificent ideals, was nothing but a "scrap of paper"; the New Covenant would work because it was to be written on men's hearts.

Doubtless Jeremiah hoped that this oracle would find its fulfilment in the little community which was gathering round Gedaliah at Mizpah. If so, he was doomed to yet another disappointment, and the murder of his friend must have seemed to him the end of his real ambitions for his people. The spiritual life of Israel was to be continued, not down the line of the few poor folks who were left in

[1] *Cf*. viii. 8.

the land, but amongst those who were now far away in Babylon. And centuries were to pass before the full meaning of Jeremiah's thought was to break upon the world. For there was one feature in the case which he had failed to enunciate. That was the medium whereby this new law was to be communicated. For leather or papyrus, ink would do; for clay or wax, the stylus. But the only instrument which would impress the truth on men's hearts was *blood*. And so, for the full realisation of Jeremiah's message, the world had to wait till that night when Jesus, having supped, " took the cup also, saying, This cup is the New Covenant in my blood." There is no fulfilment of the highest truth the Prophets had to offer, apart from the Cross.

XI

THE EXILE : EZEKIEL

IN a certain sense the Exile meant for Israel the greatest spiritual experience through which a nation ever passed. At the moment, no doubt, it appeared to be an appalling tragedy, a blow from which the people probably would never recover. It was not merely a political calamity, it was also a religious one. This is clear from the general feeling of the time, and from the theology of ancient days. If the writer of Pss. xlii., xliii. was one of the captives taken to Babylon in 596 (as he may well have been), he accurately reflects the feelings of the best men of Israel in his day. He is suffering from physical danger, he is undergoing the disgrace of slavery, he has to endure the taunts of his captors. But none of these things is to be compared in his mind with the yet more terrible thought that he is being for ever separated from his God, that he will never see the face of Yahweh again. For right down to the exile, men still clung to the old conception of territorial limitation in regard to God.

This is too obvious to be missed in the early history. The escape from Egypt has as its excuse and its aim the meeting with Yahweh at His home in Sinai. He could not or would not come to Egypt, so Israel must go to Sinai. The Song of Deborah—perhaps the oldest memorial of

Hebrew poetry that we have—represents Him as coming from Sinai through Seir.[1] When David is exiled, he describes his enemies as saying to him " Go serve other gods."[2] He is to flee to a land where Yahweh holds no sway. When Elijah seeks new strength, he goes far away to the south to Horeb, the Mount of God, and there meets with Yahweh.[3] Naaman, wishing to worship Yahweh in the land of Rimmon, has to take with him two mules' burden of earth—a portion of Yahweh's own land, on which he may erect an altar and do sacrifice.[4] It is true that to some extent, at any rate in southern Israel, Yahweh was localised in the Ark, which had given many proofs of a power dwelling within it, especially amongst the Philistines. And when the Ark found a permanent home in the Temple erected by Solomon, it was only natural that to a large extent this building should be regarded as His new residence. It is possible that the short dominance of the Deuteronomic law had done something to strengthen this feeling, though it would be unsafe to attribute any very great influence to the reform, at any rate after the death of Josiah. But, be that as it may, there can be little or no doubt that the rank and file of those who were carried away into Babylon felt that they were leaving not only their old home and their kindred, but also their God.

Then came the miracle. They discovered by practical experience that their God was there in Babylon with them. Above all, His presence was manifest in the phenomena of prophecy. There seem to have been in Babylon, as in Jerusalem, many Ecstatics, who were constantly coming before the people with their message. Yet, in all probability, they were no more reliable, and stood no more in the direct line of the development of the faith of Israel than did the popular and patriotic Prophets in Jerusalem. Jeremiah, at least, had reason to denounce them.[5] And Ezekiel is the

[1] Jud. v. 4. [2] I. Sam. xxvi. 19. [3] I. Ki. xix. 8.
[4] II. Ki. v. 17. [5] *Cf.* Jer. xxix. 8.

only one of the Prophets of the early years of the captivity whose work has come down to us as canonical. In this respect also, his position is somewhat analogous to that of Jeremiah.

The Book of Ezekiel offers us a new phenomenon, though one which had been to some extent foreshadowed in the case of Jeremiah. The Prophet's words take a definite literary form under his own guidance. A part of the utterances of Jeremiah were dictated by him to Baruch, but only a part. The larger portion of the oracular matter in the book that bears his name has clearly been preserved in much the same way as the work of Amos and Hosea. But it appears that Ezekiel was his own amanuensis, and that he not only committed his messages to writing, but, if one may use the term without implying too much of the modern sense, " edited " it. The result is that a large part of the book is in prose form. There are poetical passages, but they bear the stamp of artistry far more than any oracle which we can safely attribute to any of the great pre-exilic Prophets, and we are justified in believing that Ezekiel meant them to appear as definitely composed poems. The rest has been adapted from the original oracular form, and in this respect bears some resemblance to the prose sections of the Book of Jeremiah which are in the first person, though the general style is not so clearly Deuteronomic.

The arrangement is interesting. There is some pretence at a real chronological order, though this is far from being carried through accurately. But there are distinct signs of an attempt at grouping according to subject matter, though in this respect Ezekiel has not advanced nearly so far as the later compilers of the prophetic books, such men as those responsible for the present arrangement of Isaiah, Amos, and Jeremiah. Ezekiel does not, for instance, place together chs. xvi. and xxiii., as a later compiler would probably have done. But in two cases he has preserved large, more or less homogeneous, groups ; that consisting of

oracles dealing with foreign nations (xxv.-xxxii.) and that
which depicts the restored community (xl.-xlviii.). In these
sections it may well be that the connection was chronological as well as material. It should be added that the
text is often corrupt, but can frequently be restored with
the help of LXX, which diverges a good deal from the
Hebrew text, though by no means so widely as in the case of
Jeremiah.

Ezekiel's oracles are divided into groups of varying length,
some of them fairly long, some of them very short indeed.
At the head of each of these groups there stands a date,
which may certainly be taken as that of the oracle which
immediately follows, and as the *terminus a quo* for the rest
of the section. In one case at least the dating is intended
to be very exact, and is emphasized. The first date given
is that of the Prophet's call—592 B.C., five years after he
had been carried to Babylon with Jehoiachin. Ch. viii.
begins the next group, and is dated in the following year.
Ch. xx. is dated 590; ch. xxiv., 587; ch. xxvi., 585;
ch. xxix., 1, 586; xxix., 17, 570; xxx., 20, 585; xxxi., 585;
xxxii., 584; xxxiii., 21, 585; and xl., 572. The ministry of
Ezekiel, then, extended over a period of twenty years,
and during that time he was charged with the responsibility
of carrying Yahweh's message to those of his fellow-countrymen who were exiles in Babylon. Like his great predecessors,
however, he was far from being blind to the importance of
the events which were taking place about him. Whilst his
main care was always his own people, he was aware of the
effects of the great world movements on other peoples.
In one or two cases, notably in those of the smaller states
of Palestine, he was in some degree actuated by a knowledge of the treatment Judah had received from them, but
in all he foresaw the meaning and issue of the triumphant
march of Nebuchadrezzar. It may be remarked in passing
that his attitude towards the Babylonian conqueror was
by no means bitter, and in one instance—xxix. 17-20—

appeals to the reader as distinctly friendly. It was clear to him that the minor tribes, Ammon,[1] Moab,[2] Edom,[3] and the Philistine cities[4] would soon fall under the same yoke as Judah, but Babylon was to claim yet greater victims in Tyre[5] and Egypt.[6] Against the last two especially Ezekiel seems to have felt strongly.

One striking feature of his work was the prohibition of speech. The oracles committed to him during the last years of Jerusalem, from 592 to 585, must have been written down, and it was only after the news of the fall of the city reached Babylon that he was given free permission to utter his message aloud. In the meantime, most of the direct communication which he had to offer was given in symbolic action. This he seems to have used more than any other of the canonical Prophets. Thus he draws a picture of a siege on a tile,[7] lies for long periods on one side, eating the scantiest rations,[8] shaves his head,[9] all to typify the sufferings of Jerusalem during the siege, and digs through the wall on his house, by this vivid pantomime portraying the attempted escape of Zedekiah from the doomed city.[10] He also describes things in parables. Such is the story of the eagles in ch. xviii. and of the lions in ch. xix. It is worth noting that these are real parables, or rather almost fables, and are very different from the nature-similes of earlier prophets. The nearest parallel from any of the predecessors of Ezekiel is to be found in Isaiah's Song of the Vineyard.[11]

Ezekiel lets us see more of the character of the ecstasy than any other Prophet. In his case the principal physical effect was not that violent activity which we observe in the Prophets of Baal on Carmel, or in the Prophets of Yahweh at Gibeah. It is, indeed, the exact opposite. The muscles are constricted, and it seems that the body became

[1] xxv. 1-7.   [4] xxv. 15-17.   [7] iv. 1-8.   [10] Ch. xii.
[2] xxv. 8-11.   [5] xxvi.-xxviii.   [8] iv. 9-17.   [11] Is. v. 1-7.
[3] xxv. 12-14, xxxv.   [6] xxix.-xxxii.   [9] v. 1-4.

rigid, the whole condition resembling that of the trance.
There were doubtless other external manifestations of what
was taking place, but the phenomena described are such
as to have led some students to think of him as the victim
of disease—epilepsy or some similar affliction. His own
statement that this was always the " hand of Yahweh "
which was upon him, or the " breath of Yahweh " which
carried him to and fro, makes it clear that whatever the
name modern medical science would have given to this
condition, it was regarded in Ezekiel's day as possession,
inspiration, ecstasy. Further, the experience of the second
consciousness is exceptionally clear and detailed in his
memory. There does not seem to be the least doubt or
hesitation as to the reality of the experiences which he
recalls. He really does see Yahweh on that blazing throne-
car whose machinery was the living power of the Cherubim.
True, he is extremely cautious in his description, and can
only say what the things were like, not what they were,
and whilst he clearly recognises Yahweh himself in human
form, he makes no attempt to sketch his features. He really
is transported to Jerusalem,[1] where he beholds the abominations which are now being carried on by those whom he
had known, and who now filled the highest offices in that
Temple where he had once himself been a priest. More,
he sees Yahweh Himself, in all His glory, taking His final
departure from the city, and leaving her to the fate of her
sins.[2] So too, in later years, one cannot doubt that the
marvellous vision of the Valley of Dry Bones[3] and the
whole of the picture of the restored city and community
were as real to him as the facts of his ordinary life.

We have no data as to his age. His latest utterances
are dated 570 B.C., and if he were fifty at that time he
would have been just twenty-one when taken into captivity.
He may have been ten years younger or ten years older ;
the fact that he became a widower in 585 makes neither

[1] *Cf.* viii. 3, xi. 1, etc.   [2] *Cf.* Ch. x.   [3] Ch. xxxvii.

limit impossible, though, as there is no record of his marriage, it may be held more probable that this event took place in Jerusalem, and that he was born in the reign of Josiah. But this is merely conjecture. It is, however, clear that he was familiar with the buildings and ritual of the Temple, and there is a hint that he resented the Deuteronomic regulation by which the " Levites," or priests of the old local sanctuaries, were placed on an equality with the faithful sons of Zadok.[1] Of the conditions under which he and his fellow exiles lived in Babylonia we know almost nothing, but there is reason to believe that they formed some kind of self-governing community, for they had " elders," who do not appear to be merely respected because of the position they had held in the Homeland.[2] In spite of the favourable comparison which Jeremiah draws between them and those who were left behind,[3] the exiles do not seem to have maintained a much higher standard of morality and religion than the remnant. Ezekiel, at least, found enough to rebuke in them, and his principles forbade him to blame them for the sins of their fathers or their contemporaries.

For seven years the silence imposed on him at the beginning was maintained, and was broken only when the fall of Jerusalem was imminent. The capture of the city itself was preceded by almost the only incident of a personal character which the book contains. His wife died. He had loved her tenderly, and it was a terrible blow to him. Yet here, too, the demand of his service was laid upon him, and he was forbidden to mourn or lament for her. His action was to be interpreted in a symbolic manner. A yet greater blow had fallen on the people, and they too were forbidden all outward signs of grief. He was a portent to them, that when their sorrow fell on them they should do as he had done. There is something unspeakably tragic

[1] xliv. 10-14. [2] xx. 1, etc.

in this momentary lifting of the veil that at other times the Prophet always kept over his inner heart. He has left us no record of struggles or of passion such as those which made the life of Jeremiah a burden to him, but here we catch a single glimpse of the truth that he too was human, that he too had the power to suffer, that he too could love— and that all this must be at the absolute disposal of his God.[1]

There is one feature of Ezekiel's early life which it is impossible to miss. Before the disaster which sent him into exile, he had certainly heard the words of Jeremiah and they had made a deep impression on him. Not infrequently he seems to take a text from Jeremiah, and preach a sermon of his own upon it. There is no escape from the conviction that Ez. xxiii. is based on Jer. iii. 6-18. He repeats the proverb familiar to the older Prophet, which tried to shift responsibility on the shoulders of past generations by saying "The fathers have eaten sour grapes, and the children's teeth are set on edge."[2] It seems likely that Ez. xxii. 17-22 was at least suggested by the oracle in Jer. vi. 27-30. In Jer. vii. 16 the Prophet is forbidden to pray for his people, because Yahweh will not listen. Ezekiel is told[3] that the prayer of the holiest and the most fervent of men would avail no further than to save themselves; as intercession it would be valueless.

There is, perhaps, one other external influence which has had its effect on the work of Ezekiel. This is that element in the priestly legislation which to-day goes by the name of "The Law of Holiness," and is to be found, in the main, in Lev. xvii-xxvi. That there is some connection between this section of the Law and Ezekiel is generally agreed, but the precise nature of that connection is obscure. It is sometimes held that Ezekiel is the earlier of the two, and that this portion of the code was based upon his teaching.

[1] xxiv. 15-24.   [2] xviii., Jer. xxxi. 29. 30.   [3] xiv. 12-20.

Others believe that he was familiar with it in his early years, in other words that it was pre-exilic. Probably the truth will be found to lie between these extremes, and in the end it will be held that Ezekiel was acquainted with this legislation in an earlier and perhaps shorter form than that which it now has. The question is discussed in every good Introduction to the Old Testament.

Though Ezekiel was a contemporary of Jeremiah, and, as we have seen, had probably learnt much from him, there is a wide difference between the two men. The younger man is far less lovable than the older. There is a harshness, almost a brutality, about Ezekiel, which contrasts unfavourably with the tenderness of his great predecessors. He reminds us more of Amos in tone, carrying the air of the judge upon the bench, himself far removed from the sin he denounces and the suffering he foretells. He has relatively little of that sense of the agony of God over human sin which is so marked a feature of Hosea. To him it is horrible, ghastly, loathsome, but it does not break God's heart. It may have been his priestly training or it may have been his own temperament which made him thus, but the fact is beyond dispute. We may compare the initial vision of Ezekiel with that of Isaiah—himself not the most tender of men. To both is given the message of destruction, inevitable and complete. Yet if we set Is. vi. 9-13 alongside of Ez. ii. 2-5, we feel that the former takes up the burden with a sense not merely of weakness, but of positive pain, which does not strike us so strongly in Ezekiel. Nothing, it is true, could be stronger or more terrible than the denunciations of Hosea, Isaiah, and Jeremiah, but the passion which inspires them is that of desperate love and loving despair. Ezekiel cannot see the sinner for the sin ; his horror at the iniquity of his people blinds him to all else.

Yet even so, he sees one supreme and sublime purpose in all that Israel and other nations suffer. It is that they

" may know that I am Yahweh." This is a step whose importance it is difficult to exaggerate. Earlier Prophets had rightly seen that the sufferings which Israel had endured were intended to call her attention to Yahweh and His will, but the idea of Yahweh as the supreme God who was to be worshipped and acknowledged by others is certainly not obvious in Ezekiel's predecessors. That such a position should eventually be reached was inevitable from the day when Amos proclaimed Him God of universal morality, but the mind of man is slow to draw a fresh deduction, and it is well to mark the point at which each new thought becomes explicit. The double experience, the contact with a wider world and the sense that Yahweh's presence reached away out to Babylon, may have been the exciting cause, or the truth may have come home to the Prophet independently of any meditation on the circumstances, but the fact is there. Henceforward Israel has a world message and a world mission. Her God was no longer the tribal deity of a little hill people in a western Asiatic state ; He was the supreme end and the highest goal of human knowledge.

Yet one cannot help the feeling that Ezekiel's conception of Yahweh does not rise so high as that of some of his predecessors. There is in his presentation something which suggests the rigidity of a machine. There are certain laws of Divine action ; that is not to be doubted. Yahweh is just : that is beyond dispute. But one may well ask whether those laws and that justice are most satisfactorily represented in a God who distributes life and death with so little feeling. Ch. xviii., especially, may be the Law, but it does not read like the Gospel, and the usual prophetic tone is much nearer to the Gospel than to the Law. The stress is to some extent external. Men's actions are the criterion rather than their hearts.

Closely linked with this is the Prophet's doctrine of responsibility. He gives us the impression that he delivers

his message, not as others would have done, in the hope
of awakening repentance and winning men to salvation,
but because it would be his fault if they failed because
he had not warned them.[1] By his utterance he could shift
the burden off his own shoulders on to theirs, and for
himself he would have nothing to fear. He would have
" delivered himself." Now it is of the highest importance
that a man with the prophetic gift and the prophetic call
should feel a deep sense of his own responsibility. He of
all men cannot afford to be negligent or slovenly in his
work. But at the same time it is surely a lower standpoint
which stresses the danger to the Prophet himself, rather
than the peril of those who are about him, which appeals
to his instinct for self-preservation rather than to his pity
and yearning for the souls of men. It is the former stress
which Ezekiel feels, the former appeal which comes home
to him.

It is possible that this desire to be rid of responsibility
was due to a certain sense of the pitilessness of Yahweh.
We have already had occasion to note what must indeed
be obvious to every reader of the Old Testament, that
the conception of a loving God is comparatively late, and
even in the pre-exilic Prophets by no means universal.
A good instance of this feeling is furnished by the belief
in Yahweh's habit of misleading men through the prophetic
gift and utterance. This has already appeared in the case
of Jeremiah, but Ezekiel puts the case still more strongly.[2]
Again, one has the feeling that this man knew that he was
personally safe. Yet more terrible to the mind that has
learnt of God through the Cross of Christ is the view that the
horrible syncretistic practices of the Hebrew people,
especially infant sacrifice, were due to the direct will of
Yahweh.[3] They had revolted against Him, and He would
punish them. In order that the penalty might be as heavy

[1] *Cf.* iii. 13-21, xxxiii. 1-6.   [2] *Cf.* xiv. 9.
[3] *Cf.* xx. 25, 26 ; also Rom. i. 24.

as possible He had taught them to commit yet more iniquity, till they reached a point at which He might justly pass the supreme sentence of national destruction. This doctrine is not peculiar to Ezekiel. With it may be compared the hardening of Pharaoh's heart, and the fattening of the heart and the weighing down of the ears of Israel of which Isaiah spoke.[1] But nowhere else is the teaching carried to such lengths of terrible logic. Almost equally savage is the refusal of Yahweh to listen to the sinner.[2] To Ezekiel—and this, it must be confessed, is found elsewhere in the Old Testament, though it is far from being universal—the first attempt to bridge the gulf cleft by human sin must be from man's side. Repentance must precede grace. How different from the attitude of Him who said, " I came not to call the righteous but sinners."

Yet this very mechanical justice contains within it the seeds of hope. Whilst it is true that sin will lead to suffering of the most awful kind, it is equally true that the man who turns from his iniquity and seeks Yahweh will find a pardon which will be expressed in prosperity. Herein Ezekiel is nearer to the Prophets of the South than to Amos and Hosea. He, with all his harshness, never lost sight of the possibility of repentance, and indeed of its practical certainty. Whilst it was true that the wicked must perish, it was equally true that if he repented he would be saved.[3] The same rigid law which meant destruction to the one meant deliverance to the other. To the Prophet there were no variations and no exceptions. Apparently he found that the Exile was gradually having its effect, and that the generation born in Babylonia was avoiding much of the evil of their fathers. Consequently, as time went on, his thoughts turned more and more to the restoration and the restored community.

---

[1] *Cf.* Is. vi. 10.   [2] *Cf.* xiv. 1-5.
[3] *Cf.* xviii. 21-23. 27-29 ; xx. 30-44, etc.

To this subject is devoted the whole of the last fifth of the book. Chs. xl. and onwards describe the arrangements which he expected and desired in the new state. First of all the Temple must be built (xl.-xlii.). Then, and apparently not till then, Yahweh would return to His old home. The need for the preparation emphasizes what has already been noticed, the demand for human activity before God will step in. He will not come to Jerusalem till Jerusalem has made ready for Him. Then follow the arrangements for sacrifice and other forms of ritual (xliii.-xlvi.). One feature of the reorganised community has often been noticed. This is that the name of " king " is avoided, the civil head of the community being called " prince " or " chief." It is possible that this is due to a feeling that the monarchy was in itself a barrier to a true religious national life There was a danger that the secular power might claim supremacy over the spiritual, as had, indeed, been the case in pre-exilic times. In Ezekiel's scheme for an ideal Israelite constitution there was to be no doubt that the ecclesiastical authorities were to be the dominant power in the State, and that even the civil ruler must be subordinate to them. It is also possible that the Prophet did not contemplate the fall of Babylon or any kind of national independence in secular affairs, thinking of the restoration as still leaving Judah politically subject to Babylonia. In that case the mention of a king would be inconsistent with the actual position. His comparatively sympathetic attitude towards Babylon has already been noted, and he may well have avoided a term which might imply disloyalty or revolutionary aims.

This constitution, essentially hieratic, being completed, Ezekiel turns to the land itself. At once he sees an entirely new feature, a great river miraculously produced, going out from Jerusalem south-eastwards and growing broader and deeper as it went on, till finally it healed and sweetened the Dead Sea itself. It is difficult to decide whether this is to be taken literally or metaphorically. It is, however, more likely that the Prophet meant to imply that there would arise from the sanctuary a stream of blessing that would irrigate the most arid portions of the earth, bringing the knowledge of God to those who were most in need of it. If the literal interpretation be accepted, then we have a picture of a miracle in which prophecy is very near to the border of apocalypse. Finally the land is portioned out between the tribes, again in a purely mechanical way, and without regard to the natural features. Each tribe has a straight strip, some to the north and some to the south of Jerusalem. In the middle strip, which contains the capital itself, are the priests. It is worth noting that Ezekiel is not satisfied with the return of Judah alone. He has before him continually in these restoration prophecies the recovery of the tribes which the Assyrians had scattered a century and a half before. Not only were they to be restored, but Israel and Judah were to be united once more into a single people. One of his symbolic actions illustrates the new conditions.[1]   The new geographical scheme assumes it from start to finish, and includes, further, tribes like Reuben and Simeon, which had disappeared centuries ago, and are not even mentioned during the whole period of the monarchy.

Harsh, unyielding, and mechanical as Ezekiel's teaching may appear to be, it thus contained the very message that was needed for his people in Babylon. The line of Divine revelation was to be continued through this nation now in exile They were some day to return to their own land, and there once more proceed on their long slow task of preparation for the supreme manifestation of God in Jesus. As they were before the exile, they were utterly unfitted for what lay before them. The message of the Prophets had failed as yet to bring them back to a sense

[1] The joining of two pieces of wood, xxxvii. 15-28. *Cf.* also such passages as xxxix. 25-29.

of what Yahweh really required of them. Ezekiel with all his fierceness did reinforce the great lesson of their suffering; Yahweh was a pure and righteous God, and nothing but purity and righteousness would satisfy him. It was inevitable that there should arise the feeling that the national sins of Israel were too great for forgiveness. Under the old view of the solidarity of the people in their relation to Yahweh, a solidarity which bound together the successive generations as well as the men of each period, the awful magnitude of the iniquity of the past would be a burden which could neither be borne nor removed, and Israel's guilt could only be expiated by her complete and final destruction. Against this hopelessness Ezekiel sets his individualism, and offers to the people the opportunity of returning to their land, and making a fresh start, if those who came after him would but avoid the spiritual perils of their ancestors. It was not too late, it was never too late, while God and man endured, for them to come once more together, even when the case seemed to be so absolutely irremediable as was that of Northern Israel.

Finally Ezekiel may fairly be regarded as the father of Jewish legalism. The law and its rigorous observance have in some quarters been felt to be a declension from the high spiritual levels of the Prophets, and so, in a sense, they may have been. Yet Israel had to pass through terrible experiences before the consummation of her faith was come, and it may well be doubted if she could have withstood the flood of heathen persecution which threatened her in the second century B.C. unless she had had some external standard to which to cling. The seed of truth was there, and the function of the Law was to provide a rigid shell which should protect the kernel till the time of its sprouting.

XII

THE PROPHETS OF THE RETURN

THE empire founded by Nebopolassar and his son, whilst one of the most brilliant in history, was but short-lived. In 561, Nebuchadrezzar was succeeded by his son, Evil-Merodach, or Amel-Marduk. Two years later he fell a victim to a plot which placed his brother-in-law, Nergal-Sharezer, on the throne. In 556 his son, Labasi-Marduk, succeeded him, to be assassinated in turn after a reign of nine months only. The new king, Nabu-na'id, was the last of the Chaldean sovereigns. A fresh power had arisen in the world.

This was Persia. Originally belonging to the Indo-European races who had moved southwards some centuries earlier, the Persians were the inhabitants of the wilder mountain country to the east of Babylonia. For long under the yoke of the Medes, with the coming of Cyrus they threw off their allegiance, and secured, not only their own independence, but also dominion over their former masters (549). Cyrus then faced towards the north-west and subdued Lydia, finally turning his attention to Babylon. An attempt was made by the son of Nabu-na'id, Belshazzar by name, to meet the new enemy, but he was defeated on the upper waters of the Tigris. The king himself did nothing except attempt to get the gods into safety, and his futile religiosity resulted only in the bloodless capture of Babylon by Cyrus, 538 B.C.

These events produced a remarkable effect on the mind of Israel. The comparative acquiescence which marked Ezekiel's attitude towards the Babylonian conqueror was a thing of the past. It may be that the successors of Nebuchadrezzar were less wise in their dealings with the captive peoples. But, whatever be the cause, there can be no doubt of the bitterness which ran all through Jewish thought and feeling. They would welcome any enemy who should succeed in humbling the power of the mistress of the world.

This vindictive passion was bound up with the hope that the new master would restore the people of Israel to their own land, and enable them once more to take up the threads of their national life. And these two thoughts, the punishment of Babylon and the deliverance of Israel, found expression in a great outburst of prophecy. The oracles of the last years of the exile must have been delivered within a comparatively short time, and there is no period in the history of Israel which produced so much in proportion to its length. Prophecy of this period is nearly always easy to recognise, where it is found in our Old Testament, and it includes some of the noblest heights of thought, spiritual insight and expression that even the Prophet-poets of Israel produced. Yet—and this phenomenon is probably without parallel in literature—*the whole is anonymous*. It is in a remarkable degree self-contained and apart from what preceded and from what followed. One needs no very highly developed critical faculty to realise that it is impossible to attribute all the prophecy of this period to a single author. What has been handed down to us is the work, not of one, but of many, and yet we do not know the name of a single one of these Prophets. It is true that the ancient writers and singers of Israel were in no way anxious to perpetuate their names, and seldom called attention to their own identity, but in the case of the Prophets others were anxious to do what the original speakers did not want to do for themselves, and the greater Prophets are in some cases historically important apart from their oracles, as well as through them. Of the Prophets of the last years of the exile there is certainly one whose individuality does most strongly express itself through his message, and there are passages of rare beauty and truth which must have come from others, but while we know the men, we do not know their names. These are lost to us for ever.

As has been already remarked, in one case the work of a single Prophet does seem to have been collected and kept together. This now forms the second of the three volumes which, perhaps accidentally connected in the first instance,[1] are now bound up together as our present Book of Isaiah. The portion which is usually held to be exilic is chs. xl.-lv. But there are other sections even in the Book of Isaiah which are generally regarded as coming from this period. Such are, possibly, xi. 10-16, xiii., xiv. 1-22 (though it should be stated that there is no general agreement as to the date and reference of the great taunt-song over the death of the tyrant), xxi. 1-13, xxxiv., xxxv. There is a whole group of these oracles in Jer. l., li., though in this case the collection seems to have been made at random, and contains a good deal of fragmentary matter, and pieces of very different degrees of value and power. The closing verses of the present Book of Amos may come from the same period, and there are probably other still shorter pieces scattered through the prophetic books.

Through all these passages, whether collected or isolated, there runs the double thought, the fall of Babylon and the restoration of Judah. This is, perhaps, most evident in the

---

[1] This is almost certainly true of the attachment of ch. xl. to xxxix., but it is quite possible that the appending of lvi. *ff* to lv. was deliberate.

collection attached to the Book of Jeremiah. Duhm, who regarded these two chapters as a single whole instead of a compilation of floating oracles, complains of the number of times these two *motifs* occur, as producing an intolerable monotony of expression. As literary criticism this is hardly valid, for the oracles are not a unity, nor, probably, are they by the same author, but it serves to illustrate the dominance of these two ideas over the prophetic mind of the time As a matter of fact there are one or two passages of real beauty and power. Such are the dirge over Babylon in l. 23-27, and the pathetic attempts of her children to cure her wounds, li. 8-9.

Several of the exilic passages in Is. i.-xxxix. reach a high literary standard. Ch. xiii. is an extremely vigorous series of oracles, which has almost the appearance of a strophic poem. Ch. xiv. contains one of the most striking poems in Hebrew literature, the " dirge " or taunt over the fallen tyrant, who is in the text identified with the king of Babylon. The reference has been questioned, but there does not seem to be any decisive reason against it. One difference between ch. xiii. and xiv. is that the former deals with the people and the latter especially with the king. But it appears to be a king who has been slain in battle, either in fact or in prospect. Nabu-na'id certainly avoided this fate, and if the reference is to him, the whole must be treated as a statement of what the Prophet expected. The personal hostility to the Babylonian monarch, however, is too obvious to be missed, not only in this but also in other passages. In view of the attitude of Ezekiel it requires some explanation. It is not impossible that this may be found in the religious policy of Nabu-na'id, who definitely aimed, almost from the beginning of his reign, at centralising all worship in Babylon itself. So thoroughly was this policy carried out that Cyrus was able to pose as the rescuer and champion of the gods of Babylonia, called by them to restore them to their ancient temples. It may well have been that this policy involved an attempt to secure uniformity of worship throughout the country, and that this brought him into conflict with the more devout Jews of the prophetic party, who had at last learnt that their God was supreme. Hence both the destruction of the Babylonian power and the liberation of the people were regarded as acts of Yahweh through the Persian king. Cyrus represented himself to Babylon as the chosen deliverer of Marduk ; the Jewish Prophet saw in him the chosen deliverer, not indeed of Yahweh, but of Yahweh's people.

This, and much else, is brought out in the work of the greatest of these unknown prophets, whose oracles have been preserved for us in Is. xl.-lv. That these chapters are in the main due to a single author is generally admitted.[1] They are apparently composed of a number of different oracles, but they have been arranged with unusual skill, and, as far as ch. xlviii., and possibly further, with an eye to historical sequence. Thus they give us a picture of the last days of the Babylonian empire from within, though the attitude of the writer is unfriendly to the dying power. They open with a message of comfort for the exiled nation, strengthened by the assurance of Yahweh's universality and supremacy. There follows a somewhat vague and misty picture of the coming deliverer, whilst a contrast with the heathen gods—who are mere nothings—is repeatedly drawn. At last, at the end of xliv. and the beginning of xlv., the deliverer, the Anointed of Yahweh— the " Messiah "—is named ; he is none other than Cyrus the Persian king and conqueror. Then in a few swift sentences the religiosity of Nabu-na'id is sketched, and the reader has a vivid picture of the great gods being lowered from their temples and loaded on to donkeys' backs, to be transported to some place of safety. Next comes the

---

[1] The description of the idol factory in xliv. 9-20, and a few isolated verses in chs. xlvi. and xlviii. are sometimes assigned to another hand. The question of the " Servant Songs " is on a different footing.

entry of the triumphant army into the city, and the sense that Babylon in her turn is to be enslaved. Finally, ch. xlviii. closes with an appeal to the captives to accept the freedom that is offered to them, and to return to their own home. The dangers of the desert journey will be non-existent for them, for " Yahweh hath ransomed his servant Jacob." The remainder of the collection, in so far as it has a direct historical reference, depicts the exultation of Jerusalem on the recovery of her children.

A brief historical sketch is wholly inadequate to represent the brilliancy and the charm of a prophetic collection which has held the attention and gripped the imagination of later ages almost more than any other portion of the Old Testament. The style in which these oracles have been preserved is in itself of the highest order. No other Prophet shows such a combination of smoothness and passion. Amos is fiercer and colder ; Hosea and Isaiah are more allusive and cryptic, especially the former ; Jeremiah is plainer, and has an entirely different method. The whole of these chapters forms one magnificent outburst of joy. This in itself is a feature unique amongst the Prophets. It is not that there is here any denial or even neglect of the great moral truths that earlier Prophets have stated. Sin is sin, and just as terrible to this man as to any of his predecessors. Indeed, there is hardly anywhere a stronger condemnation of moral iniquity than that which is implied in xliii. 22-28. Yahweh's love has laid no burdens on Israel. On the contrary, it is Israel who has loaded her God. Not merely has her sin inflicted exhausting toil upon Him, it has positively *enslaved* Him. It has deprived Him of all the rights that belong to personality, it has made it impossible for His will to have free course, it has brought suffering and pain upon Him. The very fact of His love for this wayward and sinful people has in a terrible sense doomed Him to degradation and agony. The full meaning of this truth only became clear for the world to see when Jesus Himself died the death of a criminal and of a slave.

The other features of the Divine character as displayed by the Prophets also appear. Yahweh is righteous. This means in the mouth of this Prophet not merely that He will always adhere to His own principles of moral rectitude, but the phrase carries with it something of its original forensic sense. All moral and spiritual words have somewhere behind them a concrete basis, and this is one taken from the processes of law. Whenever a case arises in the courts, there are two parties. One of these will in the end win, and the other will lose. The former would be described in Hebrew by the word usually rendered " righteous," and the other by a word usually rendered " wicked "— terms which had originally a purely legal sense, and only later had a moral significance imported into them. So " to justify " in the first instance meant simply " to give a verdict in favour of," and " justice " implied not merely moral rectitude, but also success. This feature of Yahweh's justice must be remembered if this Prophet's language is to be fully understood. The liberation of Israel and the punishment of Babylon meant not only an exhibition of Yahweh's character, but also an illustration of His judicial power.

So the other elements in His nature, familiar from the teaching of earlier Prophets, are likewise brought out. His love has shown itself in many ways, but nowhere so conspicuously as in the redemption of Israel. There is a kind of wild abandon[1] in the way in which Yahweh moves heaven and earth to rescue Israel. He is the universal God, the God of all nations, but He freely sacrifices other peoples for the sake of the one which He has specially chosen and called for Himself.[2] The triumphant march of this world-conqueror would lead him to subdue all that had ever

[1] *Cf.* Is. xlii. 10 *ff*, xliv. 23 *ff*.   [2] *Cf.* xliii. 3, 4.

owned the sway of Babylon, and much more, but all this was permitted, or rather ordained, in order that Yahweh's own nation might win their freedom.[1] The miracle of love and power was as great as that which had wrought the deliverance from Egypt ages ago.

Supreme in history, Yahweh was also supreme in nature. "The creator of the heavens and of the earth" is one of the stock epithets which the Prophet applies to Yahweh. But Yahweh's power over the physical world is not merely that of an original creator. The Prophet's doctrine is no mere Deism. Yahweh can and will control, modify, and supersede the existing order of things, if that be needed. Instead of the long journey up the Euphrates valley and through Aramean territory, there will be a great causeway straight across the desert itself,[2] and Israel shall walk along it, suffering neither from drought nor from human foes. The dry waste shall be full of rivers and wells, and there shall be an abundant supply of water for all who need it.[3] Physical strength shall be given to the returning exiles, and more than merely physical strength. Should the ground prove impassable, a new power of movement will be bestowed on Israel, and they shall grow wings which enable them to vie with the flight of the loftiest birds, the very vultures themselves.[4]

There can be no doubt as to the source whence these wonders come. For Yahweh Himself, *and He alone,* has foretold them. None could have guessed them, for they are too strange, but He has known them from of old, for He has planned and brought them to pass. Others, gods included, are challenged to emulate Yahweh's predictive feats, but all are silent. He alone knows what is to come. for He alone has planned it.[5]

From this there followed another truth, which, though implicit in much of the work of the earlier prophets, and

[1] *Cf.* xlv. 1 *ff.*   [2] *Cf.* xl. 3 *ff.*   [3] *Cf.* xli. 18 *ff*, xxxv. 6, etc.
[4] *Cf.* xl. 31.   [5] *Cf.* xliii. 9, xli. 21-24.

occasionally suggested or hinted at, comes here for the
first time into its true position as one of the fundamental
doctrines of Israel's faith. The reason why the other gods
are unable to reply and accept the challenge is that they
do not really exist. They are nothing—less than nothing.
They have passed beyond the vanishing point of reality.
Yahweh no longer stands as He did to early Israel, as the
national God, one amongst many. He is not even merely
a more powerful God than His fellows and rivals. He is
the only God. There are no others. There are figures,
statues, images, which the men of Babylon had believed
to represent genuine spiritual and personal beings. But
the last calamities of Babylon had shown that after all
there was no reality corresponding to them. They were
images of phantoms conjured up by men's own thoughts
and desires, and when the things of wood and stone were
carted away from their temples, the wearied animals were
dragging along all that there was of divinity in them.
Yahweh alone survived,[1] and henceforth to the true
Jewish mind, He would stand for ever as the one living
and true God.

It is impossible to overestimate the importance of this
discovery. About this time there was springing up in Asia
Minor the early school of Greek philosophers, who were,
in Anaxagoras, Socrates, and Plato, to reach the highest
intellectual level that human thought has yet attained.
They did deduce from the laws of pure reasoning a doctrine
not dissimilar in externals from this monotheism of the
Jewish Prophets. But the latter are as far as possible
removed from the metaphysical speculation of Greece.
The prophetic faith was the simple logic of common sense,
applied to the facts of history, and still more to an interpretation of that history in the light of the doctrine of the
righteousness of God. It is characteristic of Jewish thinkers

[1] *Cf.* xlvi. 1-2.

that, whilst they reached conclusions—*e.g.*, monotheism and, ultimately, the idea of a life after death—which are found elsewhere in the philosophy of the pagan world, they reach them along a unique road. It is not the pure reason which guides them, it is the practical reason, and their basis is essentially ethical rather than metaphysical. This means that they are able to develop their doctrines from the standpoint of real personality, and thus they utterly avoided the pantheistic snare which lies in wait for those who seek to evolve a theoretical monism from intellectual abstractions.

Embedded in the collection of this Prophet's oracles is a series of poems which all deal with one subject, a certain Slave of Yahweh. The poems are xlii. 1-4, xlix. 1-6, l. 4-6, and lii. 13—liii. 12. It may safely be said that no section of the prophetic literature has been more closely studied or is more generally known than these four short passages. They have been universally—or almost universally—interpreted as Messianic in Christian circles, and there has been unlimited discussion as to their exact origin and meaning. Where the reference is not held to be Messianic, at any rate in the first instance, there have been a number of theories put forward as to the original from whom the portrait has been drawn. It is impossible in an outline sketch such as the present to give any account of these suggestions ; it will be necessary to confine discussion to the more obvious and superficial features presented by the poems themselves.

In the first place it would appear that they are all the work of a single poet, and possibly not the Prophet to whom we owe the rest of this collection. It is not merely that there are resemblances in style between themselves and differences which they share when compared with adjacent passages. Such arguments, though they have a certain validity, and may be valuable when used to reinforce others, are seldom of the greatest weight except in extreme cases. It is true that no serious reader of the Hebrew Bible can fail to be conscious of the difference in style between, say, Genesis i. 1—ii. 4 and the narrative which follows. But there is no such striking contrast here, and if style, language, and vocabulary were all we had to go upon, there would be little justification for assigning them to a different author. Of far greater importance is the view that is taken of their subject. They all deal, apparently, with a " Slave of Yahweh," and describe his call, his labours and his sufferings. Now the expression " Slave of Yahweh " or " My Slave " is one of the characteristic phrases of the whole collection. But, outside these passages, it is always applied either to Cyrus, or, more commonly, to the whole people Israel. In these four passages it can be neither. It is certainly not the Persian conqueror, and the " Slave " is more than once definitely set over against the rest of his people. This is not clear in the first passage, where the mission of the slave is to the Gentiles. But it is unmistakable in the second, where the mission is stated as having been at first to Israel and afterwards extended to the wider world. In the case of the third, again, it does not appear; but in the fourth it is practically certain. It is, of course, possible that scholarship has been misled in grouping all four together, and that they should be regarded as unconnected ; but it must be admitted that the evidence is in favour of their unity.

It would seem, then, that the compiler found these four passages—" songs " they are commonly called—and fitted them into the oracular material which he was working into a volume. Certain it is that whilst none of them is closely attached to what precedes it, each of them, except the last, runs smoothly—one might almost say dissolves— into what follows. So much is this so that different commentators have disagreed as to the end of one or two of the songs.

They have marked variations amongst themselves, particularly in the way in which the Slave himself is introduced. In the first song the speaker is Yahweh, who describes His own purpose and the character of the man whom He has chosen to do His work. In the second and third it is the Slave who speaks himself, and tells of his call and something of his own experience. In the fourth the Slave is dead, and his story is told by men who saw and watched him while he lived, joined in the general hostility to him, or at least regarded him with indifference, but now at last realise who he was and what his mission has been. This variation is by no means incompatible with a regular historical sequence, and on the whole lends strength to the view that all are by a single poet who desired to depict the full course of the life of his subject.

Whether that subject was a real person must remain in doubt. It has been supposed that the writer had before him the story of a historical individual—Isaiah, Jeremiah, or Zerubbabel. Others have believed that the fate of Israel as a whole amongst the heathen nations is in view ; others, again, are inclined to hold that the conception is that of an ideal nucleus of genuinely spiritual Israelites who suffer as this Slave does amongst their more materialistic countrymen. But one cannot help feeling that whilst details may be suggested by the sufferings of some unknown individual—perhaps of more than one— the whole picture is no more that of an actual historical character than was Glaucon's sketch of the perfectly just man in Plato's *Republic*. What is brought before our eyes is the character of the ideal slave of Yahweh, of the man who is utterly and wholly devoted to his Divine Master, who has " poured himself out, even to the point of death."

Such a man is definitely called and trained by Yahweh for his task. From the moment of his birth, and even before, he has been set apart for it.[1] The same solicitous care

[1] xlix. 1.

has guided him through his early life.[1] Yahweh has watched
over him, steadily shaping him into fitness for the supreme
task that is to be his. It is no rough work that lies before
him ; only the finest tool will accomplish the purpose of
God. So he has been polished, smoothed, refined, and
when prepared has been laid aside and cared for till
the moment for effective action has come. And still the
Presence is with him. He has been trained to listen for the
Divine voice, and every morning its utterance comes to
his ear. Even at the end, when the worst has befallen him,
Yahweh justifies him, and proves to an incredulous world
his ultimate triumph by apportioning to him a share in
the spoils of the mighty.[2]

This means that his task has been definitely achieved.
The purpose for which he was chosen and prepared has not
been left unfulfilled. His methods have been novel, but they
have been effective. Instead of open and blatant pro-
clamation of his message, his demeanour has been one of
modesty and tenderness. The ordinary Prophet was
expected to do spectacular things, and the incidence of
the ecstasy was such as to rouse interest and attention by the
commotion which it caused. The Slave's weapons were
far other than these. Quietness and peaceful, retiring meek-
ness were his characteristics. He would not beat down oppo-
sition, nor would he discard the frail and damaged tool. If it
were light that he sought, he would be content with the lamp,
even when it was on the point of expiring for want of oil.
If it were music that he tried to win, he would make the
best even of the cracked reed that another would have
crushed and flung aside. Yet his tenderness was that of
strength, and not that of weakness. His light was always
clear and pure ; his tone was always rich and full. For his
aim was to establish righteousness, and true righteousness
can be established in the last resort only by means which
have no element of violence in them.[3] And, be it noted, the

[1] xlix. 2 ff.   [2] liii. 12.   [3] xlii. 2-4.

righteousness which he seeks to enthrone amongst men
is no mere forensic victory ; it is a deeper thing. It is
interpreted in the fullest sense as a national covenant, not
simply a covenant between one nation and another, but
between a whole nation and its God.[1] It involves a real
conversion of the people, an opening of their eyes and a
liberation of their souls. There are times of depression
when it seems that the task is too great and that the labour
can only end in failure. Yet it is just then that there
comes a vision of a wider purpose, and there rises before
the worker the still grander prospect of a redemption
which is not confined to his own people, but shall embrace
the whole of fallen human nature.[2]

Thus in very truth his life itself becomes a sin-offering.[3]
Just as the slaughtered victim burnt upon the altar removed
the barrier which human wrong had raised between
the finite spirit and the infinite, so by the free surrender of
life and of all that makes life precious in the eyes of men
this Slave wins the power to make intercession for
the transgressors.[4] There is only one way in which life
can be won for men : that is, through death. He alone
who ruins himself can find himself, and the fullest form of
self-realisation is in the altruistic triumph of an unselfish
redeemer. It is no wonder that the Christian Church has
seen that the complete fulfilment of this prophecy has
only been attained in Jesus, whom men delight to call
"the Lamb of God, which beareth away the sins of the world."

It goes without saying that such an aim is not achieved
without pain. And it is as the " Suffering Slave " that this
ideal has been known to later generations. That suffering
is of no ordinary kind. It involves disease. Though he
may have no human friends, there is one acquaintance who
never leaves him, who is always on his doorstep, who shares
the privacy of his home and chamber. That intimate is
sickness.[5] It is, too, a disfiguring sickness, for his face is

[1] xlii. 6.　　[2] xlix. 4-6.　　[3] liii. 10.　　[4] liii. 12.　　[5] liii. 3.

not beautiful. The sight of him awakens no chord of
affection ; there is no attraction there. On the contrary,
his visage is spoiled so that it is no longer a man's ; his
form is marred out of all human likeness.[1] Either for this
reason, or because of some possible pollution, he dare not
show himself to men. He is " as one who hid his face
from us,"[2] and a veil is before his countenance, so that
those rotting features cannot be seen. In a word, he is
" one under the stroke,"[3] and reason and philology alike
point to leprosy.

The figure changes. Not only is it that of a victim to
the most terrible disease known to man, it is, perhaps in
another individual case, that of the persecuted saint. He
has committed no crime, yet men avoid him. In making
their calculations they leave him out of account, even when
they do not actively despise him.[4] But they are not satisfied
with rejection and scorn. He suffers actual insult with a
lofty patience, and " hides not his face from shame and
spitting."[5] His enemies will go to any lengths. On a false
and trumped-up charge he is dragged before a lawless
court, and is condemned as a criminal of the deepest dye
on perjured evidence by an unjust and tyrannical judge.[6]
His sentence is the last that a human bench can inflict,
and he suffers the extreme penalty of the law. Even death
does not end the persecution, and his foes wreak a senseless
vengeance on the lifeless corpse, and fling the carcase into
the pit where the bones of the common criminals moulder.
" He made his grave with the wicked, and with evil-doers
his tomb."[7] The picture which Plato sketched a century
and a half later has already been filled in.

He is not ignorant of the meaning and purpose of his
passion. He knows, though perhaps vaguely, that he is

> " By the pain-throb triumphantly winning intensified
>   bliss "

---

[1] lii. 14, liii. 2.   [2] liii. 3.   [3] liii. 4.   [4] liii. 3.   [5] l. 6.
[6] liii. 7, 8   [7] liii. 9 ; this is probably the original reading.

—not for himself, but for others. And he has thereby thrown a great flood of light on that mystery which men call the Problem of Suffering. It is necessary to be careful in speaking of this question, because it would not be true to say that we have set before us a solution of that problem. That may be for ever beyond the reach of human intelligence. But there is something here which offers relief from its pressure, at least in certain cases. There is in some strange way a redemptive value in all disinterested and undeserved pain. It is still possible to ask where the justice lies in allowing the innocent to save the guilty at such cost to themselves, or why the salvation of the sinner should be purchased only at the price of the agony of the sinless. Yet it is worth realising that to the sufferer himself, if he be the genuine Slave of God, the compensation is adequate. For there are moments of vision, when the immediate outlook is at its blackest, in which a sense of the truth comes home to him, and he *knows*. With that perfect self-surrender which is the primary condition of his service, he can look out over the years and see the line of those who are in the deepest spiritual sense his children, those with whom he has travailed, and for whom his pain has won life. And with this insight into the eternal reality his own problem and his discontent disappear. He suffers, but they live, and in their life he finds his own. He may not reason the thing out ; in the fact he recognises the highest justice. He may not be able to explain it ; he can do better, for he can feel it. Knowing that, he makes many righteous and bears the burden of their iniquity.

" Away out of the agony of his soul he seeth,
    He is satisfied by his knowledge."[1]
For him, that is enough.

[1] liii. 11.

XIII

PROPHECY IN THE RESTORED COMMUNITY

IF one may judge from those of his oracles which have come down to us, the greatest difficulty experienced by the Prophet of Is. xl.-lv. was not the hostility of the enemies of Israel, but the apathy of her own sons. They had come to accept the situation, and to be prepared, as far as one can judge, to endure whatever was laid upon them by their captors. It may well be that the new spiritual light that the Exile brought with it contributed to this result. Israel had realised for the first time that her God was universal, that He was no mere local deity, but the Creator and Lord of the whole universe and of all humanity. It was inevitable that with this expansion of God there should come also the sense of the insignificance of the Hebrew nation and still more of the Hebrew individual. Yahweh was the shepherd of the stars, and knew them all intimately: how was it possible that He should care for one small and crushed nation ? It was only too natural that she should feel that her way was hid from her God[1] and that her case had been passed over by Him in favour of larger and more important communities. Hence the Prophet's repeated exhortations to comfort, his repeated insistence on Yahweh's special

[1] Is. xl. 27.

interest in Israel, and his repeated appeal " to come out from among them " and return to the widowed city of their fathers.

In recent years it has been held by some students that there never was any real return from the Exile, and that the new community which continued the national life and faith was composed of the relics left by the Chaldean invasion in 585. Whilst this view has not found general acceptance, it seems clear that the permission of Cyrus to return to their own land was not widely accepted by the Jews. They had taken the advice of Jeremiah and had settled down. They had good homes, and, apart from possible persecution on religious grounds, were on the whole not badly treated. Commerce and perhaps agriculture engaged their energies, and it was not easy for them to sacrifice an established position. Some, no doubt, did take the long journey, and made the sacrifices, but there must have been many, perhaps the majority, who preferred the comfort and safety of exile to the hardships of travel and new colonisation. Those hardships must have been considerable. The Jews had enemies who had to some extent profited by the desolation of Judah, and were unwilling to see her in any real measure restored. Life was more difficult, agriculture more uncertain in the doubtful climate of Palestine than in the richly irrigated land of Babylonia. Reconstruction after a colossal disaster always seems a slower and more arduous task than the upbuilding of a new society on an entirely fresh basis. Trade was not easy, for Jerusalem has never been one of the world's great natural markets, as Damascus and Samaria were. The inevitable result was that during the first twenty years of the Persian period the high hopes of the Prophet were not realised. So far from being a country of wealth, happiness and prosperity, Judah was a land in which bare existence could be won only by constant struggle and unremitting toil.

There is a veil over the first eighteen years of the restoration. We have no records whatever of this time beyond the bare fact that a certain Sheshbazzar[1] was the " prince " of the new Judah ; for what is recorded in Ezra i. and ii. of Zerubbabel and Jeshua is probably to be thrown forward into a second expedition which aimed more expressly at the rebuilding of the Temple. Whether this be so or not, it is clear that no effective steps were taken for many years even to restore the sacred edifice. The death of Cyrus was followed by the reign of Cambyses, and his assassination plunged the empire into a confusion from which it was only rescued by the triumph of Darius over the pretender, Smerdis. The new monarch did not belong to the royal house, but justified his elevation to the imperial throne by his ability as an administrator. It was to him that the Persian power mainly owed the strength which enabled it to endure for two centuries.

Early in his reign there arose a new prophetic movement in Jerusalem, which is known to us through the prophecies of Haggai and Zechariah. The oracles of the former are only four in number, and are all dated in or about the year 520. They were reduced to writing (in prose form) apparently by the Prophet himself, and the correct dates prefixed. All are addressed either to Zerubbabel or to the Priests, though the rest of the people are at times included. All are to the same purpose, the rebuilding of the Temple.

Haggai evidently found that the greatest difficulty was the reluctance of the people themselves to do the work which lay to their hands. The arguments he uses are interesting, if only as showing the change which had passed over the spiritual life of Israel. He cries shame on those who are living in good houses themselves whilst the house of Yahweh lies still in ruins. He promises that there shall be supernatural evidence of the power and activity

[1] Ezra i. 8

of Yahweh,[1] and threatens drought and similar disaster
if the will of Yahweh is not done.[2] Such calamities have
already occurred, and are due to this neglect. Further, till
the Temple is built, there can be no ritually pure offerings.
There is something very like an interdict upon the people,
which will remain till they are ceremonially restored in
the erection of the new sanctuary.[3]

It is difficult to imagine a greater contrast than that
which appears between the Prophet of Is. xl.-lv. and Haggai.
There is no longer a really spiritual message. Even the
denunciations of sin and corruption which had marked the
utterances of the pre-exilic Prophets are wanting, and
the Prophet seems to have included stone and timber
amongst the essentials of his spiritual and religious ideal.
The demands of Yahweh are indeed changed, and the
change will be found to be characteristic of most of the
post-exilic prophecy.

If one is less conscious of this declension in Zechariah,
it is partly, but only partly, because he presents his case
with greater power. It should be noted at the first mention
of his name, that it is not possible to regard the whole of
the material included in our present Book of Zechariah as
the work of the same Prophet. The original book extends
only down to the end of ch. viii. It is clear that some
accident has occurred, similar to that which attached
Is. xl. ff. to the original Book of Isaiah. It would seem
that when the prophetic collection was completed, the
Book of Zechariah was the last of the named Prophets
in the series. There followed three anonymous oracular
collections, each bearing at the head the phrase " Massa
d⁰bar Yahweh "—" The burden of the word of Yahweh."
One of these—the last of them—had a pseudo-personal
title extracted from its text (iii. 1), and has ever since
been known under the name " Malachi "—" My Messenger."

---

[1] ii. 6, 7.   [2] *Cf.* i. 10, 11, etc.   [3] *Cf.* ii. 10-14.

The other two, though of a very different character from the third and from the prophecies of Zechariah, were simply allowed to run on from the latter book, and were not unnaturally regarded as part of it by later ages.

In thinking of Zechariah, then, we have to deal only with chs. i.-viii. The greater part of this is composed of visions, probably seen in the ecstatic state and described afterwards by the Prophet. As is usual where the Prophet was his own amanuensis, or himself arranged for the writing of his oracles, the original poetic structure (if these ever had any) has been obscured, and the whole is in prose. Two dates are assigned to the visions, indicating the years 520 and 518 B.C., though it is by no means certain that all the visions which follow the former date are necessarily confined to the day stated. The visions themselves are unique in character. The first[1] is a picture of Yahweh Himself, standing in a grove of myrtles, and receiving reports from all parts of the earth. The second[2] describes four horns, destroyed violently by four smiths. There follows closely the picture of a surveyor,[3] who marks out the generous dimensions of the city to be newly built. Next comes a celestial trial scene,[4] in which the High Priest appears as defendant, charged by the Satan, or Public Prosecutor of the Court of Yahweh, and acquitted by the Judge Himself. Then a golden lampstand,[5] to which it seems a later writer has attached two olive trees whose living strength supplies a continuous flow of oil. A winged scroll[6] flies from the land, bearing away the curses which have hitherto hung over Judah. The sin of Judah is embodied in a woman who is placed in a large vessel closed with a heavy leaden cover. and carried off by two winged women.[7] Four chariots are seen,[8] each drawn by horses of a different colour, and in the last scene[9] a golden diadem is made and placed on the head of Joshua the High Priest.

[1] i. 7-8.   [2] ii. 1-4.   [3] ii. 5-9.   [4] Ch. iii.   [5] iv. 1-7.   [6] v. 1-4.
[7] v. 5-11.   [8] vi. 1-8.   [9] vi. 9-15.

These visions are presented to the reader with extraordinary literary skill. The scenes are vivid, and, when once we have freed our text from later modifications—sometimes absent even from the LXX's text—they are clear and simple. We see things as the Prophet saw them, and feel as he felt. There is an atmosphere about the stories which marks the writer as an artist of the highest class. This is perhaps most noticeable in the first vision, where one finds oneself actually present, and looking through the dimness to where the central Figure stands, shrouded in a gloom which prevents His features from being recognised. But this same power of atmosphere is manifested elsewhere. The trial is thoroughly dramatic, and in none of the narratives does the prophet fail to impart the impression of the scene.

The visions do not exhaust the surviving oracles of Zechariah. Prophetic material of the more familiar kind appears in ii. 10-17, and in the last two chapters, in all these cases exhibiting the normal features of the dictated or written oracle as contrasted with the type which is publicly uttered. A study of these passages, as well as of the visions, reveals the fact that Zechariah was much nearer in temper and in outlook to his great predecessors than was Haggai.[1] Whilst he was at least as eager as his contemporary for the establishment of the theocratic government of Judah on a proper basis, he recognised the fact of Yahweh's moral demands[2] and was far from regarding the ritual of the sanctuary and the ceremonial law as constituting the essence of religion.

He was certainly not indifferent to the national welfare. He was as much Judah-centred as was Jeremiah, though without the passion of the great pre-exilic Prophet. That he knew of Jeremiah's work and was desirous of endorsing it is obvious from his reference to the covenant formula.[3] He

[1] That Haggai, too, was not entirely indifferent to the principles of the earlier Prophets is clear from the close of his book.
[2] *Cf.* vii. 8 *ff.*   [3] viii. 8.

looked forward also to a considerable extension of the city, and an expansion of her power. There is a suspicion that he was prepared to go yet further, and was amongst those who dreamed of seeing her once more completely independent of foreign power. This, at least, seems to be the meaning of the coronation of Joshua,[1] and it may well be that he expected to find in Zerubbabel, not merely a governor under the Persian king, but a sovereign prince who would cast off the alien yoke. Certainly the disappearance of Zerubbabel from the history of Judah is one of those things which have never been explained, and it may well be that he was suspected of treason against the Persian court and removed in disgrace, possibly seriously punished. If that were so, it may well be that part of the responsibility rests on Zechariah.

Yet to Zechariah, as to the great pre-exilic Prophets, political matters were only a minor consideration. We feel, as we read him, that we hear again the old call to the service of a righteous God. If we are tempted to look with some superiority on the narrowness and local patriotism of these Jewish Prophets, it behoves us to remember that they stood —and to a large extent realised that they stood—in a unique position. Their theology was narrow-minded, it may be ; but had it been otherwise they could never have accomplished the task that lay before them. It is easy for us to be tolerant, for we live under conditions for which the theological battle has been won many centuries ago. We are no longer—at least in Europe—faced with a religion or with groups of religions which are often no more than organised systems of iniquity. We are not accustomed to justify crime if it is committed in the name of religion ; we rather condemn a religion in whose name crime can be committed. But in the days of the Persian Empire it was not so. The little people of Judah stood alone amongst

[1] There is some doubt as to the text, and it was possibly Zerubbabel who was crowned.

the nations of the world in their insistence on a pure ethical monotheism. Even the Persians themselves had failed to accept the best things in the teaching of Zarathustra, and Cyrus in his inscriptions shows himself to be quite as thorough a polytheist as any Babylonian monarch. It was on the Jew and on the Jew alone that there fell the whole weight and responsibility of the new creed which was ultimately to win supremacy wherever men sought the knowledge of God.

Thus it was necessary that such men as Zechariah should, for the time at any rate, be narrow and nationalistic. But with all that, he feels intensely the horror and the weight of sin. That is clear from the vision of the Woman in the Ephah. And the sins are not merely failures to observe due ritual. Whilst Zechariah is as anxious as Haggai to see the Temple rebuilt, he does not charge it to Judah as a crime that she has left the edifice incomplete. Rather it is a misfortune, and one of those which Yahweh Himself will remedy. The real sins for which she suffers are the old social ones—injustice, falsehood, oppression, and the like. Zech. vii. 8-14 (which seems to be a mutilated fragment of some longer passage) reads like Jeremiah. It is because of such wrongs as these that Judah was carried away captive, and it is because they have not yet been wholly abandoned that she still remains in partial desolation. If she has failed to achieve what she sought, it is because her courage has failed, and she has not given to Yahweh the co-operation which He needed to fulfil His purpose concerning her. She has thought success too miraculous for her ; it has therefore been too miraculous for Him.

There is thus a very real affinity in tone between Zechariah and the Prophet of Is. xl.-lv. For in the main the oracles of the former, like those of the latter, look forward to a time when all the trouble will have passed away, and Judah will enjoy full prosperity of every kind. It is true that the trouble is different. It is no longer oppression in a foreign

land, with the constant pressure of the heathen world :
it is weakness, folly, sin, and desolation in their own
country. But there is still the ideal, still the marked failure
to achieve it, and still the promise and hope of a brighter
day to come.

As with the pre-exilic Prophets, this brighter day can
come only with a genuine spiritual revival. Of that revival
the rebuilding of the Temple and a measure, possibly, of
political independence are but the outward signs. For even
while Zechariah urges Zerubbabel and Joshua to achieve-
ments as yet beyond them, he does not ask them to rely
on material means. It is " not by might nor by power,
but by my spirit, saith Yahweh,"[1] that the true Jews'
hopes are to be consummated. No army large enough to
defeat the Persian forces, no mass of wealth or other
material power is to win for them the victory, but the
direct activity of the Spirit of God. A successful revolution
is always in the last resort a spiritual one.

The history of Israel for the next eighty years is almost
a complete blank as far as the record of events goes. Yet
the prophetic impulse was not dead, and as the years went
by there still rose men from time to time who have left
some record of the message that their God gave through
them to their people. It is almost impossible to assign
any accurate date to them, and they are all nameless. For
the most part their work has been attached to that of
earlier Prophets, or included within other compilations.
There may well be notes and short oracles belonging to
this period (which ends with the coming of Nehemiah to
Jerusalem and the establishment of the Law under Ezra)
scattered through many of the prophetic books, but there
are in the main two collections or groups of oracular matter
which are later than Zechariah and earlier than 444.

These are the group contained in Is. lvi.-lxvi., and the
book which now bears the name of Malachi. It is not

[1] iv. 6.

necessary to discuss here at length the reasons which have led most modern students to regard the former as a distinct collection ; they can be gathered from any good technical work on the subject. Suffice it to remark that the whole situation is different from that presupposed by the great Babylonian Prophet of xl.-lv. Judah is now at home again, and is mainly under the government of her own people, though there is no mention whatever of a " king." The Temple is standing, and apparently has long been standing. Still more remarkable in this connection are the differences in outlook. The last chapters of the Book of Isaiah deal with the same kind of problem as those which confronted Ezra and Nehemiah—though at times the conclusions reached are not identical. In a word, the most suitable historical background, as far as we know the history of Judah, is the generation which immediately preceded the governorship of Nehemiah.

At the same time it is difficult to maintain that all the oracles included in this collection are from the same Prophet. There is no positive evidence to the contrary, but there is no continuity of thought, no great single idea worked out through the whole. A large variety of themes are dealt with, and there is no strong evidence of unity. The group forms really a miscellaneous collection of oracles which have comparatively little in common, save the fact that they come from the same period and reflect the same general outlook.

The new note is struck at once in the first few oracles in Is. lvi. These lay a stress on the keeping of the Sabbath[1] which has appeared only once before in a passage in the Book of Jeremiah,[2] whose originality is doubtful. Now the importance of this piece of ritual observance is so great that even the foreigner and the eunuch who desire to enter the commonwealth of Israel may do so, on condition that

[1] lvi. 1-7.   [2] Jer. xvii. 19-27.

they observe this one regulation. Yet the observance of the Sabbath is not to be a merely formal thing. It is true that it is to mean refraining from doing one's daily work, and from pursuing one's own pleasure. But that is only a means to an end. The true end of the Sabbath is that it is to be a day in which Yahweh and His people can really enjoy one another, when the merely material is to be laid on one side, and men are to concentrate on the spiritual.[1] This is the old prophetic tone. It is heard again in the matter of fasting.[2] It must be remembered that in all religions and amongst all peoples in the East, fasting has been and still is a regular and genuine religious exercise. The Oriental does find that abstention from food enables him to concentrate more readily on the non-material and spiritual, and to him fasting is a recognised " means of grace." It is noticeable that in the great passage which deals with fasting, the Prophet does not condemn the theory or the exercise. What he does is to offer a truer conception of what the fast should be than that which was currently held amongst his people. It is not to be a time when men shall merely afflict themselves. The reader is reminded almost inevitably of the remark of Jesus about men who disfigured themselves to let their friends know that they were fasting. The true fast is to be a day of real self-denial and self-forgetfulness—a day when their pity, mercy, and charity can overflow to others, and their hunger is to be produced, not by methods which will reduce their own expenses, but by giving to the needy the satisfaction of their normal wants. Once more one finds the genuine and nobler attitude of the pre-exilic Prophets. There is no attempt to do away with what is already well established, but rather to glorify it with a new spirit, in which the humane character of the God of Israel can be fully manifested.

[1] lviii. 13-14.   [2] lviii. 1-12.

There are other features in which the Prophet (or Prophets) came nearer to the message of the pre-exilic Prophets than to that of the great exilic one. There is, for instance, a much fuller recognition of sin, not merely as of something that is past and atoned for, but as something that is still present and is threatening the life of the modern community. There is denunciation of the social and economic sins, oppression,[1] injustice in the administration of law,[2] falsehood,[3] and sexual impurity.[4] There is a full recognition of the fact that these things will inevitably bring sorrow with them or after them,[5] but also of the more important fact that the real danger involved in them is that they cut men off from God. Yahweh's great triumphs are not won. It is not His fault, it is theirs, for it is their iniquities which make it impossible for Him to do all that He could and would.[6]

There are other sins which are of a more strictly theological cast. There is the attempt to build a new Temple somewhere, which may be a reference to the Samaritan Temple on Mount Gerizim.[7] But the arguments used would suit any attempt to centralise worship and confine it to a particular spot, for they are based on the universality of Yahweh. He is everywhere, and made the world; how then can He be confined within the walls of any material building ? But there are darker features than this in the worship of Israel. It is clear that the return had failed to make any deep impression on the country at large. It is possible that the peasants had absorbed a large Canaanite element, and it seems to have been in the villages that the old habits of worship lingered longest. Those who were left behind after the fall of Jerusalem would appear to have retained their old habits and outlook. There were ritual forms, such as the ancient sacred dance,

---

[1] Cf. lvii. 1.   [2] Cf. lix. 14.   [3] Cf. lix. 15.   [4] Cf. lvii. 3, etc.
[5] Cf. lvii. 10, lix. 1-11, lxv. 11-15, etc.   [6] Cf. lix. 2.
[7] lxvi. 1 ff, sometimes also connected with the Temple at Leontopolis.

and various types of sacrifice and sacred meal which had perhaps never been wholly swept away, even by the Deuteronomic reform.[1] These have survived the re-establishment of the Temple, for the returned Jews seem to have concentrated on the city life, and left that of the country to the men who were there already. But, as in days of old, this cannot be tolerated, and some of the most vigorous oracles of the collection are directed against what are rightly seen to be ritual abominations. Again we have the old attempt to purify the religious life of Israel.

But the oracles in this long group are not confined to Judah's sin. There is also the hope of pardon and prosperity. In fact the larger part of the collection is concerned with the restoration of the Prophet's own people. There are enemies round about Jerusalem, who are to be defeated and destroyed. In this triumph it is Yahweh Himself who is to be the supreme actor, and our Bible contains few more terribly splendid passages than that which describes His return from their overthrow.[2] Men have been helpless, so He has risen in His might and has trampled down His enemies as grapes are trampled in the winepress. So He comes, with swift and stately tread, his garments stained and reddened—but not with wine. The traditional pronunciation of the first verse of the passage identifies the enemy with Edom, whose savage fury in 586 had never been forgotten by the Jews. But the words rendered "from Edom" and "from Bozrah" may also be pronounced so as to mean "reddened" and "more than a vine-dresser"—

" Yonder—who cometh becrimsoned ?

Stained deeper his robes than a vintner's "

—which would make the reference more general.

There is more in this prospect than the merely vindictive recoil of the oppressed. Elsewhere, though the same vivid fury appears, it is subordinated to the thought of the

---

[1] lvii. 3 *ff*, lxv. 1 *ff*, lxvi. 17 *ff*, etc.   [2] lxiii. 1-6.

deliverance of Israel. This appears, for instance, in the famous passage imitated from the Slave Songs of Is. xl.-lv., which Jesus applied to Himself in the synagogue at Nazareth.[1] Vengeance is mentioned, but the main thought is deliverance. At times we see clearly that those who have returned to form the new community are only a small part of the nation, and that there are yet many who are still in foreign lands, probably held under some form of restraint. Thus there is language in lvii., 14 ff. which recalls the great appeal and message of the Babylonian Prophet. A similar reminiscence is to be caught in lxii. Jerusalem is still suffering from the effects of her sin, but the glory of Yahweh is soon to be hers, and will carry with it a moral supremacy and a spiritual leadership over all the race. Especially does this note ring through the greatest of all the passages of restoration, ch. lx. There the Holy City is presented as the natural mistress of the world. Her own children are to be restored to her, and all nations will yield their service and their wealth. The primary aim is the religious dominion of Yahweh, who does these marvels for His own sake. But it is clear that the religious dominion of Yahweh involves the political dominion of His people. It is only so that real righteousness can be secured in the world. Eastern nations groan permanently under the tyranny of rapacious officialdom, but in the new state the very government officials are to be " prosperity," and justice is to be the distinguishing character of even the tax-collectors. Only those who have seen something of oriental society can realise how Utopian such a picture is. Yet even in this glorious presentation of the triumph of Israel and her God there is a darker gleam, for acquiescence is to be secured from the Gentile world by violence if necessary, and the nation and people that will not submit to be her slave will utterly perish.

[1] xi. 1-7.

From time to time with these things there are mingled prayers. There is repentance, submission, and a plea for forgiveness in lxiv., and in lxiii. 15ff. Yahweh is the true Father of Judah, but He is an ancient Father, with rights of life and death over His children, and whilst He has the Father's love, He has also the potter's power.[1] The figure is not a new one, but it is worth while noting that whereas Jeremiah[2] had used it to bring a message of hope in restoration, the later Israel employed it to express human helplessness in the hands of omnipotence. There is a new spirit in the community.

Much of what is included in this collection of prophecy is high in tone and beautiful in language. Yet we cannot avoid the feeling that there has been a real decline from the great utterances of pre-exilic and exilic days. The old appeal to righteousness is still there, but the ritual interests, which are so obvious in Haggai, are mingled with it. Israel has still a universal message, but it is the message of a universal dominion, rather than that of a universal mission. It was perhaps inevitable that this should be so. First comes the great passion, the motive force. For its own efficiency it needs to create for itself some external machinery by which it can produce its effect on the world. As time passes there is a change in the relations between the force and the machinery. They increase inversely in importance. The external grows in power, the spiritual gradually loses its hold. What was at first a means to an end becomes an end in itself. The process is gradual, and none can say with certainty where it begins. But it does begin, and it does come to a period. Then the life ebbs from it, and the spiritual progress of the race is taken up by other organisations and other forms of expression. So the old Hebrew prophecy, used by Divine Wisdom for a purpose which no

---

[1] lxiii. 16, lxiv. 8.   [2] Jer. xviii. 1-8.

other means known on earth could have achieved, lost
its primal impulse, and sank. Its peculiar task was done,
and it failed and perished. Yet its failure was not the end.
The falling torch of Divine revelation was caught by other
hands from its loosening grasp, and borne onwards till it
found its goal in Jesus.

Yet before leaving the subject of prophecy proper, there
are two other books that must be noticed. One is the
collection of comparatively late oracular matter which goes
under the name of Malachi. Reference has already been
made to it, and it is impossible to do more than glance at
its main thought. It is obvious at once that the tendency
already noted in Is. lvi.-lxvi. has become stronger,
and it is probable that these oracles were all uttered shortly
before the arrival of Ezra in Jerusalem. There is at the
beginning of the book a mention of Edom. This is not
surprising, for to the post-exilic community Edom loomed
large as an enemy. There is, for instance, a small collection
of oracles against that people, which now goes by the name
of Obadiah, and which need not further be discussed.
But the rest of "Malachi" is largely concerned with
questions which are ritual rather than moral or spiritual.
Thus the priests (who, be it noted, are the Levites, as in
Deuteronomy, not the sons of Aaron, as in the later law)
have failed to do their duty in the matter of sacrifice. The
result has been that the formal worship of Israel has been
defiled, and that in consequence the very springs of spiritual
life have been dried up.[1] Another crime, which has
resulted in drought and famine, is the failure to pay duly
the tithe of all produce.[2] A third is the habit, which men
of Judah had formed, of contracting marriages with heathen
or semi-heathen women.[3] It will be remembered that this
was one of the points on which Nehemiah and Ezra laid
most stress. The rule was probably introduced by the

[1] i. 6-14.   [2] *Cf.* iii. 8-12.   [3] *Cf.* ii. 14.

former before the establishment of the new Law, and it
must have entailed great hardship in a number of cases.
The infant churches in polygamous countries are often
faced with a similar problem, and have often felt that the
solution was to enforce monogamy as far as possible without
making the regulation retrospective. Such humanitarian
considerations would probably not appeal to a strict
legalist like Nehemiah, and this Prophet was with him.

For all these sins a certain judgment was foretold.
Yahweh would appear in the Temple, and would wreak
vengeance on those who had flouted His commands.
He would come as a consuming and devouring fire. There
would be a distinction made between the righteous and the
wicked, and it would be only the latter who would be
consumed. And finally, there would be due warning given,
for no other than Elijah would appear to announce that the
extreme penalty was at hand. Here, and perhaps here only
in the little collection, we meet with a note of mercy.
For the purpose of this newcomer would be to give men
a chance to recover. The judgment pronounced was not
inevitable, if men would listen to the messenger; it might
possibly be averted for those at least who accepted the
message.

It may safely be said that there is no book amongst the
Old Testament Prophets which more clearly exhibits the
characteristics of the decline. The very forms of religion
against which Amos had protested are now elevated to the
highest position. Hosea and Jeremiah had no use for
sacrifice, and Isaiah spoke in language which might well
be interpreted as condemning it.

Pre-exilic Prophets would not, perhaps, have swept it
away altogether; their concern was to see that men
realised that religion was a moral and spiritual thing, and
not merely a ritual one. The restoration of ritual to its old
position as the essential element in religion begins with
Ezekiel. With him the other features are, however, the

dominant ones. In Isaiah lvi.-lxvi. the same character appears, ritual *plus* righteousness. Already to Haggai Yahweh's demands centred round the Temple and its ritual, and in " Malachi " the process seems to be complete. It is not without reason that this book stands in our English Bibles as the last of the Prophets.

Once more, and that at a date which it is impossible for us to do more than vaguely guess, the true mission of Israel is expressed in a book included amongst the Prophets. This is the Book of Jonah. It is startlingly different from any other volume in the same section of the Canon. There is not a single oracle in it from beginning to end. There is no dealing with Israel or condemnation of her sin. Instead, the book consists of a narrative about the Prophet, telling how he was sent to warn Nineveh of the destruction which was to befall her, of how he shirked his duty and tried to escape to the other end of the world, how on the voyage misfortune befell the ship, and he was cast overboard, to be rescued by a great fish and restored to the dry land. Then, finding it hopeless to escape his mission, he went to Nineveh, gave his message, and sat down away from the city to observe its destruction. But Nineveh repented, and the destruction was averted. So Jonah found himself not merely baulked of the vengeance he had expected on the city which had been the terror of his people, but dis-credited as a Prophet. He had a further lesson to learn. A gourd sprang up over him and sheltered him from the burning sun. Soon it withered, and he sorrowed over its loss. Then came the supreme message of the book—" If you can pity so small a thing as a climbing plant, shall not God pity this great city, with its massed inhabitants ? "

There is no need here to comment on the stress—the unfortunate stress—that has been laid on certain incidents in the story to the practical exclusion of its real meaning and purpose. There is a Psalm in the book, which has clearly been inserted during the process of transmission, for it is hardly suitable to its present position. There have been in recent years a number of expositions which differ in detail from one another, but it is clear that in the main the story is an attempt to sketch the mission of Israel, and to some extent the spirit in which she set about her task. Thus Nineveh is the heathen world, and Jonah is the Prophet-nation of Israel. It is hers to tell the world the will of her God, and to call men to repentance. But in the very attempt to fulfil her task—and the attempt is only made reluctantly—she shows a spirit of narrow vindictiveness, and has to be taught that the universal God who has chosen her for a special purpose cares also for the other sheep who are not of that fold.

In a very real sense, then, the Book of Jonah is the forerunner in Judaism of Christianity. It was on that very question of the universality of the true monotheistic faith that the Church ultimately broke away from its Jewish tradition. It is not the three days and three nights that make Jonah the sign, it is the universality of the Gospel which the book implies. It is true that Israel never learnt that lesson, and that failure made her story perhaps the greatest spiritual tragedy in history. She abandoned her world-mission, but the Church accepted it, and for us who have succeeded to her heritage, it is profoundly true in Christ, that "there is none other name under heaven whereby men may be saved."

XIV

ESCHATOLOGY

WE have now watched the whole growth of Old Testament Prophecy. We have traced it from its seed, apparently insignificant and unworthy ; we have noticed its sudden bloom in Amos, and its ripening in his successors ; and we have seen its decay. From the time of Nehemiah onwards it ceases. It is possible that the ecstasy still appeared as a phenomenon, but it is no longer the vehicle of fresh truth. It was perhaps the most striking religious manifestation that has ever been seen, but the whole of its course was run within four centuries, and when it had done its work it declined and died.

The decline is unmistakable in the post-exilic Prophets. The great work which the Prophets had to perform was the statement of eternal moral and spiritual laws, and right down to the time of the exile it is possible to trace a real development. The picture of God grows clearer, and each one of the great Prophets has something to add to what his predecessors have said about the character of God and of His demands on men. Progress continues until the return to Palestine, but there it ceases. Of Haggai, Zechariah and Malachi, the best that we have been able to say is that they repeated the views and tried to enforce the lessons of Amos and those who followed him. This is valuable, but it is not progress. Their age, like our own, needed the message which had come through these great men of old, and the Prophet was still the natural medium through which that message was given. But by the end of the fifth century their work was practically done. It is sometimes said that Israel went into exile a nation and returned a Church. This is not wholly true, but they were well on the way to becoming a Church when they were restored to their own land, and the consummation was really achieved by Ezra. The community which resulted from the work of the great scribe was one which had grasped with absolute certainty that ethical monotheism which it was the function of the Prophets to bring home to the world. The faith had to pass through many vicissitudes in the next four centuries, but the dangers which threatened it came from outside Israel and not from within.

This does not mean that the post-exilic Prophets had nothing to add to what their predecessors had said. On the contrary there was, as we have already seen, an entirely new element in their thinking. This was the stress on ritual, so characteristic of the later Prophets, and so alien to the earlier. It was one of the features of religion which Amos, Hosea, Jeremiah, and Isaiah had most strenuously denounced, and though their attitude might have been different had the ritual been of that purer type which the Law maintained, they would never for an instant have endorsed the contention that ritual of any kind was amongst the absolute demands of Yahweh. Here the post-exilic Prophets were in the line of the development of Judaism, rather than in the full stream of the revelation of God. For the Law was one of those institutions which a more complete revelation has superseded. It was necessary perhaps for a time, but in the long run proved to be a blind road from which men had at last to return in order to find the true path to the ultimate goal. Prophecy had run its course.

and the religious life of Judah now diverges along three lines, each of which, however, may be seen to have its starting point in the prophetic writings.

The first of these is legalism. Appearing in Ezekiel, and with probably a long history behind it, it found its expression in the Law which Ezra promulgated in B.C. 444. It presents a strange contrast to the fresh vitality of the Prophets. Yet it had its uses. It served to mark Israel out as a peculiar people, and gave them the sense that they had a special possession of their own to which they must cling at all costs. Without it they would hardly have survived the close contact with the heathen world which conditioned their history from the end of the third century onwards. Under its protecting surface there did continue the genuine ethical monotheism and a deep piety which were to have their fruit in later ages.

The second line was that of the personal spiritual life. This is to be traced back to Jeremiah, and, as has been already observed, it forms the most important element in that Prophet's work—at least from the point of view of the evolution of the world's religion. Whilst there are here and there in other books touches and suggestions which show how the personal sense of God took hold of the heart of Israel, it is mainly in the Psalter that one looks for its full development. Nor can there be any doubt that its value and influence have been incalculable. Not only in the later Jewish Church, but in the Christian one which in a measure succeeded it, the Psalms have played a profoundly important part. The language of religion is to a large extent based on that of these Jewish saints, and their words are repeated in one form or another in practically every kind of Christian worship.

The third line is what we call eschatology. This has, as a matter of fact, more kinship with ecstatic prophecy than either of the other two. Both legalism and personal piety are more or less offshoots of prophecy ; eschatology is its direct development. The former have their roots in the work of individuals ; the latter, in greater or less degree, is to be found running through the whole series of prophetic writings, from Amos onwards.

For, long before the appearance of the first of the great canonical prophets of Israel, men had begun to speculate on how the world would end. There were stories and theories about its origin, and these were linked up with the final scenes. It seemed impossible to men that things should always go on as they were, and this feeling grew stronger in times of difficulty or distress. It seemed to them—and this appears to have been true of other nations as well as of Israel—that matters would reach such a pitch of rottenness that there was nothing to be done, no remedy and no cure. In such a case God (or, amongst heathen nations, a god) would appear, and end the age by violent means, vindicating Himself and establishing those in whom he delighted on a permanent basis of security. To this study of the last things, whether ancient or comparatively modern, the name of eschatology is given, and it is connected with a peculiar type of literature commonly called Apocalypse. During the prophetic period eschatology was somewhat in the background, and apocalyptic literature, if it existed at all, left little trace on the sacred books of Judah ; but when the spirit of prophecy failed, men found in eschatology its substitute and natural successor.

Our Bibles contain two apocalyptic books only—one in the Old Testament and one in the New. The former is the Book of Daniel and the latter is that of the Revelation. But there are in several of the prophetic books eschatological passages of greater or less length, and it is possible to trace a certain growth in the development of apocalyptic literature. There is, nevertheless, a marked difference between apocalypse and prophecy. Both in Israel are based on a profound belief in the power of Yahweh and His will and capacity to interfere in mundane affairs.

But in the case of prophecy the interference is always by natural or rather normal means. If calamity is to befall Israel because of her sin, it will come through drought or famine or foreign invasion—all disasters with which the ancient world was only too familiar. The apocalyptic tone is entirely different. There Yahweh manifests His power, not by the use of normal means but by interference with them. The events which are to usher in the end of the present age and the beginning of the new are not such as men have seen before. The sun is to be turned into darkness and the moon into blood. The heavens are to break open and there are to be signs and wonders such as human eyes have never beheld since the beginning of time. Especially, Yahweh is to appear in visible form, and to sweep His enemies (and those of His people) before Him in utter rout, afterwards judging the earth and rewarding His faithful ones. In all cases the things which are to happen are outside the previous experience of men.

Already, in Amos, we hear of an expected "Day of Yahweh." The context makes it clear that he was quoting a phrase which was on the lips of many in his day, and was familiar, therefore, to his hearers. Further, it is obvious that this expectation involved triumph. It was to be a day of "light," and one needs no great force of imagination to conjure up a picture of happiness and universal bliss for Israel. As we have already seen in commenting on the work of that Prophet, it was a part of the message of Amos to correct this impression, and to show that when Yahweh did appear, it would be to take vengeance, not on the foreigner for Israel, but on Israel for her sins. We are thus led to the belief that even the popular religion of Israel had an eschatology, probably derived from the Canaanite creed adopted with such disastrous completeness by the Hebrews on their settlement in the land. It is not impossible that this may be traced still further back, and that it owed its existence in Canaan to the Babylonian influence which had been dominant in Palestine from the time of Abraham, and even earlier.

But in Amos the mention of the "Day of Yahweh" is only cursory, and it would seem that the Prophet himself, so far from accepting the details of popular belief, was rather concerned to substitute not merely an altered objective, but altered methods, for practically all the disasters which he foretells for Israel are such as may be regarded as more or less normal—drought, famine, earthquake, foreign invasion, eclipse. It is, perhaps, not too fanciful to see an eschatological element in Jeremiah's great chaos-vision, iv. 23-26. But it is only in post-exilic literature that we find a real development of the subject. For the full Apocalypse the student of the Old Testament must turn to the Book of Daniel.[1] There are others which are commonly assigned to the last two centuries before the Christian era, and the series continued till some time after the fall of Jerusalem in A.D. 70. For two hundred and fifty years it was the characteristic form of Jewish literature. But the greater part of this is included in what we call the Apocryphal section of the Jewish writings, and the two books which have already been mentioned are the only separate examples in our Protestant Bibles.

There are, however, parts of the prophetic literature of the Old Testament which are certainly eschatological. The first of these is the section included as chs. xxiv.-xxvii. in the Book of Isaiah. Others are found in the Book of Joel and in Zechariah ix.-xiv. Each of these has its own character, but they all clearly belong to the same type of literature, that from which ultimately the Apocalypse proper sprang.

The section Is. xxiv.-xxvii. has long been recognised as much later than the Prophet with whose work it is included.

---

[1] Most readers will be aware of the fact that the Book of Daniel is not included among the Prophets in the Hebrew Bible. No special study has therefore been given to it in this volume.

It contains two distinct elements. The one, which forms as it were the framework of the whole, is a description of a great triumphant feast of Yahweh, in which His people share. He is proclaimed the universal King, and the feast is that which celebrates His coronation. The other element consists of various songs which celebrate the triumph of Yahweh or the destruction of His foes.[1]

The picture opens, then, with the sudden appearance of Yahweh on the earthly stage. His activities are violent and revolutionary. The very form and shape of the world is altered, for He empties it of all that it contains, and " twists its face "—so that it is unrecognisable. This revolutionary activity extends to the social world as well as to the material one. There also com plete confusion will reign. All distinctions are abolished, and all relationships reversed. The first are last and the last first, the servant and the master are no longer to be distinguished from one another. The same confusion extends to religious matters, for there is no longer any line to be drawn between the Priest and the people. It is as though all humanity had been shaken from its age-long order and organisation, and poured indiscriminately into a mortar, there to be pounded by a common pestle. The theme is then expanded. For a time the poet dwells on what has been destroyed in this overthrow. All that made life happy, pleasant and safe is gone. Especially mentioned is a certain " City of Chaos." All the analogy of apocalyptic literature tends to the identification of this city with the oppressor under whose yoke Israel was at the time groaning. Unfortunately Israel had many oppressors, and we cannot be sure which was immediately in view. For that, amongst other reasons, the date of the whole has to be left uncertain. The terror is once more

---

[1] The Songs, four in number, are as follows :—xxv. 1-5, 9-12 ; xxvi. 1-19 ; xxvii, 2-6. The remainder seems to be continuous apocalyptic narrative, except possibly for one or two verses at the end of xxvii. whose originality is doubtful.

described, and the swift violence of Yahweh closes with the gathering of all nations into a subterranean dungeon, while He prepares to ascend His throne.

There follows the great triumphal feast.[1] It is noticeable that all peoples are summoned to it, and that all share to some extent in the glory of the new time. We can only suppose that there is an implicit exclusion of the tyrants and enemies who are already imprisoned. But the new time as thus set forth is characteristic of the later aspirations of the Jewish people. There is to be a complete removal of all sources of sorrow and pain. Men had been accustomed to show their grief in times of mourning by wearing veils over their heads. These veils are now swept from them, their faces are revealed in happiness and delight, for the last of all enemies is overthrown—Death is dead. S. Paul's use of the passage in I. Cor. xv. 54 will occur to every reader.

But there is still work to be done. The wicked have not been completely annihilated, and Yahweh leaves the hall of feasting to execute His last judgment on His foes. For the moment the faithful are exhorted to hide themselves till the raging fury of Yahweh be passed. For the judgment is come. All secrets are revealed ; the earth will no longer hide the blood that has been shed upon her, and the corpses of the buried slain will appear in evidence. Above all, the oppressive city will suffer her last punishment, and the whole force of Yahweh's might will be employed for her ruin. Once more she is nameless, but is indicated under the title " Leviathan " — here (as in Job iii. 8) the primeval antagonist of Heaven, whose character and fate were well known to the ancient world. The last verses of ch. xxvii. may include a certain amount of matter due to later accretion, but the finale is clear. All evil is concentrated into the conception of Leviathan. His doom means the

[1] xxv. 6-8.

destruction of all that is bad, all that is hostile to Yahweh or threatens to hinder the accomplishment of His purpose. Now that purpose is fulfilled, and it is fulfilled in the exaltation of Israel to universal supremacy.

We may be tempted to feel that the Jewish outlook was narrow and parochial. To the mind accustomed to think of the great masses of humanity and the wide spaces of the world there is something amazingly arrogant in the claims and hopes of Israelite eschatology. Judah never had been a great people, either numerically or politically, and had, indeed, rarely been free from the dominance of some foreign power—Egypt, Assyria, Babylon, or Persia. It is almost as if one of the Indian Feudatory States were to cherish the prospect of world-wide dominion. Yet it must be remembered that Israel was a peculiar people, and that the Exile had driven into her very soul the fact of her unique position. She had met many races, and her horizon had expanded. But the more she saw of other nations, the more she realised her own apartness. All her experience strengthened her impression that the world held only two classes of humanity—monotheists and polytheists. The first class contained herself alone, the second the rest of the world. The heathen might differ amongst themselves in colour, in manners and in speech, but all their differences together did not outweigh what they had in common. All alike believed in and worshipped a multitude of gods and goddesses, and nowhere was there any successful attempt to connect principles of righteousness with religion. Israel, on the other hand, had grown out of her non-moral polytheism into an ethical monotheism, which must in the nature of the case become universal in its outlook. It is true that in her mind this lofty doctrine was bound up with her national faith, and that she still thought of Yahweh as her God, and of herself as Yahweh's people. The true universalism of the Book of Jonah was still far beyond her, and was possibly never realised by the people as a whole. Hence it was almost inevitable that her outlook should be narrow, and that it should fail to conceive of the spiritual triumph of an ethical monotheism save through her own political supremacy.

Apart from the Book of Daniel, Is. xxiv.-xxvii. presents us with the most characteristic piece of Apocalypse in the Old Testament. Most of the regular features are there— the violent interference of Yahweh in the world, His " supernatural " methods, His triumphant destruction of His foes, the universal outlook, the salvation of Israel from distress and her ultimate supremacy. In the other documents mentioned these are combined with elements which more closely resemble normal prophecy.

Thus the Book of Joel is concerned in large measure with a swarm of locusts and their ravages. Its date is entirely uncertain, though the balance of probability lies on the side of the post-exilic period. It used to be argued that its apocalyptic tone implied lateness, but we now suspect that some form of eschatology is actually earlier than canonical prophecy. Nevertheless there are frequent indications of late date, especially in the free use that seems to be made of other Old Testament writings. At the same time the apocalyptic elements seem to belong to a time when eschatology had not developed as far, for instance, as it seems to have done in Is. xxiv.-xxvii. Probably the book is to be placed earlier than those chapters, possibly in the first part of the fourth century B.C.

Commentators have disagreed as to whether Joel's locusts are real or metaphorical. To some the description of ii. 4 *ff* appeals as purely imaginative. On the other hand it is claimed by those who have direct knowledge of locusts and their capacities that the " exaggeration " in the picture is no more than a justifiable poetic licence in expression. This view is supported by the fact that the Prophet sees in the frightful calamity a call to prayer and fasting. Further, there comes the promise that the humiliation and worship on Israel's part shall not go unrewarded.

There is little in all this that can be called eschatology. The Prophet does, however, identify the locust plague with the "Day of Yahweh." He uses language which suggests that of Amos, and if we had no more than this we might well assume that Joel had seen in this disaster an illustration of the truth which Amos had tried to convey. But we have more—a good deal more, and that of so different a type as to make a reader sometimes wonder if the compiler has grouped together material which came in the first instance from more than one Prophet.

The Day of Yahweh is now in prospect. It is to be heralded by a certain number of strange occurrences. The first is an epidemic of those phenomena which ancient Israel referred to the activity of the Spirit of Yahweh. It is more than a "breath"—it is a wind, poured in sweeping storm over all Israel, or possibly over all humanity. The manifestations of the Prophet and the powers of the Seer are almost universal. Men and women, old and young, slave and free—all feel the impulse of Divine possession. Then creation turns to chaos. It must be remembered that the rarer natural phenomena, such as eclipses and volcanic action, are apt to be classed as "supernatural" by the ancient mind. So in sky and earth portents appear— "blood and fire and columns of smoke, the sun shall be turned into darkness and the moon into blood."

These events, however awful, are but preliminaries. They serve to give warning, and such as understand may use them. For from these and every other possible calamity a refuge may be found in Mount Zion. The "signs" affect all and are seen by all, but to the people of Yahweh they afford the means of escape, and even the promise of restoration. For Israel, scattered and oppressed, is collected from amongst the nations. Here (iii. 4-8) the compiler has inserted

a short denunciation in prose of the nations which had been
especially criminal in their dealings with Israel. The
picture resumes its more general aspect. Israel has now
been isolated from the rest, and on them the doom falls.
It begins with an inversion of an earlier Prophet's[1] dream
of peace—ploughshares are to be beaten into swords and
pruning hooks into spears, and the assemblage of nations
dissolves into a chaotic welter of indiscriminate battle.
Then in the general confusion of Nature, Yahweh speaks.
The language is once more that of Amos, but the thought
is far other. The purpose of the theophany is expressed in
terms borrowed from Ezekiel—that the nations may
recognise Yahweh—and His appearance marks a consummation which the eighth century Prophets certainly
never contemplated. Israel's foes are crushed, whilst not
only safety but eternal dominion are secured to the chosen
people themselves. With this contrast the book closes.

Two collections of oracular matter have been attached
to the Book of Zechariah. The first of these consisted of
chs. ix.-xi., and possibly included also xiii. 7-9. Such
displacements easily happen in the process of repeated
copying. The date of the collection is disputed, for it has
much in common with the prophecies which are connected
with the return from the Exile, whilst the mention of Greece
in ix. 13 is now generally accepted as pointing to a time
not earlier than the conquests of Alexander. It should
be remarked, however, that this merely gives a *terminus
ad quem* for the collection as a whole, and that some of the
oracles included may be much earlier. A good deal of the
material is concerned with the metaphor of the shepherd,
especially a prose section in xi. 4-16, and oracular matter
in xi. 17, xiii. 7-9. The metaphor also appears in x. 2-4.
Apart from this, the main theme seems to be the destruction
of Israel's enemies, and the recovery of her scattered exiles.

[1] Is. ii. 4 : Mi. iv. 3.

There is language which is thoroughly Messianic, but nothing that can strictly be called apocalyptic.

The case is very different with the second of these collections, comprising chs. xii.-xiv., with the exception, already noted, of xiii. 7-9.[1]

It does not seem that there is a regular succession of events expected, as in Is. xxiv.-xxvii., but the apocalyptic thought and language are unmistakable. Ch. xii. opens with a gathering of all nations to besiege Jerusalem. But Yahweh interposes, striking panic into the enemy and inspiring His own warriors to deeds of heroic valour, whereby their triumph is secured. There follows an obscure passage which in some ways recalls Is. liii. Israel has apparently done to death a hero and saint, and, later, realising his true character, bewails her own crime. Curiously enough the mourners are grouped under four "families"—David, Nathan, Levi, Shimei. If we knew for certain what this fourfold division meant, we might have some valuable light on the political and religious situation of the writer's age. All that one can suggest is that the first two names are intended to imply a civil authority and the last two an ecclesiastical one. We may guess that there is a further reference to the great Slave passages in the opening verses of ch. xiii., in which Israel is purified of three great evils—sin and uncleanness, idolatry and (of all things !) prophecy.

In ch. xiv. it seems as if the cycle were starting afresh. Once more Jerusalem is besieged, and half her people carried into exile. Again Yahweh appears, this time in true apocalyptic guise. Men flee as from an earthquake— that referred to in Am. i. 1 is especially mentioned. All natural phenomena are confounded. Day and night are

[1] It should be remarked that many scholars regard chs. ix.-xiv. as a single whole. To the present writer it seems probable that they were independent collections, which, with Malachi, were appended to the Book of the Twelve

no longer differentiated; dawn comes in the evening. Ezekiel's vision of the stream flowing from Jerusalem is recalled,[1] but with considerable modifications. There are here two rivers, one flowing eastwards to the Dead Sea, and one westwards into the Mediterranean. Then follows the punishment of the hostile peoples, crushed beneath Yahweh's stroke. Yet there is alleviation and hope. Some escape, but only on condition that they link themselves with the spiritual community of Israel. So is the world purified. All the evil is purged from it, all the good is harmonised and unified, and the picture closes with the universal peace in which the meanest things are stamped with the seal of Yahweh's holiness. A consecrated people, a consecrated race, a consecrated world—that is the end of all things.

It will be noticed that in all these cases the final consummation is expected through the intervention of Yahweh in person, and that the whole is to be completed on the earthly plane. Even in Is. xxv. 8 it is a continued life on earth[2] that is secured by the abolition of death. Later and more developed eschatology underwent a modification in both these respects. It is true that there is nowhere in the Prophets any clear statement of a doctrine of a life beyond death. There are a few passages into which that doctrine has been read,[3] but in every case the exegesis is uncertain and fails to command universal assent. There was always of course, a doctrine of Sheol, but this is a very different thing from the truer conception of immortality in which the outstanding characteristic is eternal communion with God. Yet it was from the prophetic teaching that this doctrine ultimately arose, and though not strictly apocalyptic, it must be kept in view as one of the essential elements in the final Jewish eschatology. Its history seems

---

[1] Ez. xlvii. 1-11.   [2] cf. also Is. xxvi. 19, and Dan. xii. 2.
[3] e.g., Is. liii. 10-12. This is the interpretation actually adopted by the LXX.

to have been the slow logical development of the belief in the righteousness of Yahweh.

The great question of Habakkuk and Jeremiah found no answer amongst the Prophets. The inequality in the assignment of rewards and punishments does not seem to have troubled others. Ezekiel, with characteristic dogmatism, laid down a mechanical law of retribution, and his successors seemed content to accept it. But sooner or later it was bound to be challenged again, and in certain Psalms, notably xxxvii., xlix., and lxxiii., it is discussed. It forms the main problem of the Book of Job, where for the first time there is a hint of the solution which has brought satisfaction to the mind of the Jew and the Moslem, and a large measure of relief to the Christian. That solution lies in a doctrine of a life after death, in which man can meet with God. On its purely ethical side it foreshadows the demand for another life without which the present is morally unintelligible. It had crude and even grossly materialistic features in Jewish eschatology, where (as in Daniel) we meet with a resurrection of the body. In Christianity this teaching has been modified by the application of the Greek view of a spiritual immortality. Nevertheless the Jewish doctrine of the Resurrection has this supreme virtue. It does not arise from a contemplation of the soul as an order of being, but from an instinctive appreciation of moral personality. It is not a logical conclusion reached by a process of strict dialectic, it is a truth seen in the light of earlier revelation to be axiomatic. It is not deduced from a study of man ; it is discovered through the knowledge of God.[1]

This discovery. however, was not made till after the close of the prophetic period—so slow is the human mind to realise the implications of its own beliefs. Messianic elements, on the contrary, go back to the first generation

---

[1] It should be remembered that some scholars trace the doctrine of the Resurrection to the Hebrew Psychology and to the Messianic hope.

of canonical prophecy, and possibly earlier. To the oriental mind the highest welfare of the individual and of the community can only be attained under a wise and benevolent despotism. Hence the national prosperity of Israel is bound up with the advent of an ideal king. Such a one is sketched in Is. ix., a passage which may fairly be attributed to the son of Amoz. Another Messianic passage in Is. xi. seems to be exilic, inasmuch as the language implies that the " tree " of Jesse has been cut down, leaving only a stump in the ground. Again, xxxii. 1-4 may be Isaiah's. In all these cases it is the perfect king who is expected, and there is, strictly speaking, no eschatological context, still less an apocalyptic background of thought. It is a simple human ruler of men who is in view, wise in justice, benign in administration, and heroic in military defence of his people.

Similar remarks apply to Jer. xxiii. 1-4 and 5-6, two passages doubtless associated by the compiler on the ground of their common subject. The originality of both has been disputed, but the use of the first by Ezekiel (ch. xxxiv.) seems to render Jeremiah's authorship probable. It introduces the metaphor of the shepherd for the first time in canonical prophecy, though its use in connection with monarchy goes back certainly to Micaiah, and is possibly much older. But the last calamities of the Jewish kingdom lent to it a fresh significance. The second passage, vv. 5-6, speaks of the coming king as a " branch," and suggests a reference to Zedekiah.[1]

Other references occur in passages of uncertain date, but probably all post-exilic. Thus in Mi. v. 2 the birthplace of the new king is indicated as Bethlehem. This is probably no more than a repetition of the idea that he is to come of the stock of David. In Zech. xi. 4ff. the idea of the shepherd

---

[1] The new name given to the coming prince is " Yahweh-Zidkenu," almost the same name as Zedekiah, though the two parts of it are inverted.

is expanded, and as in Jeremiah and Ezekiel, a contrast is drawn between the ideal ruler and the princes known to the Prophet's contemporaries. In Zech. ix. 9-10 his triumphant entry into Jerusalem is described, together with the extent of his dominion. In all this, again, there is nothing that is strictly eschatological or apocalyptic.

A different atmosphere is to be felt, however, in Malachi, particularly in iii. 1-4, where "he who cometh" is no longer a king, but a messenger, perhaps to be identified with the "Elijah" of iv. 5.[1] He heralds the great theophany, but is himself a terrible and almost divine person. Yet even here the apocalyptic element is far from being developed, and it remains true that through the prophetic period the doctrine of the Messiah progresses apart from eschatology. Later centuries associated the two groups of thought, and in the Book of Daniel the Messiah is a fully apocalyptic personality.

Thus in the writings of post-Biblical Judaism eschatology embraced the national expectation of the Messiah and the personal hope of immortality. There are indications of a further development,[2] and the Messiah is no longer expected as a mere man, but as a divine being. The long spiritual pilgrimage was nearly over. Jesus came. The old age ended in far other fashion than that which popular eschatology had expected. The Kingdom of God was inaugurated, yet so different was it from that to which men had looked forward, that they failed to recognise it, and by their very failure revealed its true character. For its spiritual nature and universal bearing, its moral implications and its racial salvation, its emphatic exposure of human sin and its transcendent revelation of Divine love, its earnest of communion with God and its pledge of the life everlasting— these things became manifest only in the Cross. That is

---

[1] It should be remarked that this verse is frequently regarded as a later addition to the book.

[2] *e.g.*, in the Book of Enoch.

the radiant centre of all man's knowledge of God. Up to Calvary led all the religious history of Israel; from it has flowed all the truest spiritual life of later ages. It may well be that the human race stands as yet near the beginning of its career. There may be before mankind æons of progress in the understanding of the life and death of Jesus. One thing is sure : All that came before Him led up to Him, all that comes after Him must start from Him, " that in all things He may have the pre-eminence."

FINIS

INDEX.

INDEX OF BIBLICAL PASSAGES.

REVISED BIBLIOGRAPHY
G. W. ANDERSON, F.B.A.

The literature on Prophecy is so vast that the problem of selection is particularly difficult. For this reason, and because of the special needs of those who are likely to use an introductory textbook like the present one, only works written in English and English translations of works in other languages have been included. The latter are indicated by " E.Tr." The items are numbered to facilitate cross-reference.

GENERAL STUDIES OF PROPHECY

(1) E. W. Heaton: *The Old Testament Prophets*, new and revised edn, Darton, Longman & Todd, London, 1977. A lucid and stimulating survey, giving particular attention to the vocation and the teaching of the classical prophets.

(2) C. Kuhl: *The Old Testament Prophets* (E.Tr.), Oliver & Boyd, Edinburgh, 1960. A compact but comprehensive presentation of the prophetic movement and literature in chronological order.

(3) R. B. Y. Scott: *The Relevance of the Prophets*, revised edn, Macmillan, New York, 1968. A superb account of the nature of Israelite Prophecy and the theological and social implications of the prophetic teaching.

(4) G. von Rad: *Old Testament Theology*, vol. 2 (E.Tr.), Oliver & Boyd, Edinburgh, 1965, pp. 3-315, of which *The Message of the Prophets*, S.C.M., London, 1968, is a revised form. A stimulating treatment of the prophetic movement and of the classical prophets, who are presented as having radically reinterpreted the national traditions. The author's view that Apocalyptic is linked with Wisdom rather than with Prophecy has been severely criticised.

(5) J. Lindblom: *Prophecy in Ancient Israel*, Blackwell, Oxford, 1962. An enlarged and extensively revised English version of a book originally published in Swedish in 1934. This is the most comprehensive and authoritative work on the

subject, dealing with literary, psychological, and religious problems and offering illuminating comparisons with prophets, mystics and the like, in other lands and ages, including medieval Christian mystics. There is a very full bibliography, which was enlarged in the 1963 reprint.

(6) A. Heschel: *The Prophets*, Harper & Row, London, 1962. A substantial and highly individual interpretation, concentrating on the classical prophets from Amos onwards.

(7) A. Lods: *The Prophets and the Rise of Judaism* (E.Tr.), Kegan Paul, London, 1937. Though now somewhat old, this is still a fine study of the classical prophets in their historical setting.

(8) A. Guillaume: *Prophecy and Divination among the Hebrews and other Semites*, Hodder and Stoughton, London, 1938. Since this book was published, new material about prophetic types among Israel's neighbours has come to light; but it still repays study.

(9) W. Robertson Smith: *The Prophets of Israel*, A. & C. Black, London, 2nd edn 1895. A foundation work in the modern critical study of the prophets, and a masterpiece of interpretation. Does not go beyond the eighth century.

Reference may also be made to the appropriate sections of the standard Introductions to the Old Testament and to the articles on Prophecy in Bible Dictionaries, one-volume commentaries on the Bible, and in collections of essays, in particular the following:

(10) A. B. Davidson: " Prophecy and Prophets ", in *Hastings' Dictionary of the Bible*, T. & T. Clark, Edinburgh, 1898-1904, vol. 4, pp. 107-27. In spite of its date, still of great value.

(11) J. Muilenburg: " Old Testament Prophecy ", in *Peake's Commentary on the Bible*, ed. by Matthew Black and H. H. Rowley, Nelson, Edinburgh, 1962, pp. 475-83.

(12) B. D. Napier: " Prophet, Prophetism ", in *Interpreter's Dictionary of the Bible*, ed. by G. A. Buttrick, *et al.*, Abingdon Press, Nashville, 1962, vol. 3, pp. 896-919; also additional articles by M. Buss, " Prophecy in Ancient Israel ", in Supplementary Volume, 1976, pp. 694-7, and by H. B. Huffmon, " Prophecy in the Ancient Near East ", ibid., pp. 397-700.

(13) L. I. Rabinowitz: " Prophets and Prophecy ", in *Encyclopaedia Judaica*, Jerusalem, 1971, vol. 13, cols. 1150-76.

(14) N. W. Porteous: " Prophecy ", in *Record and Revelation*, ed. by H. W. Robinson, Clarendon Press, Oxford, 1938, pp. 216-49, with bibliography, pp. 486-9. A profound study of some of the central problems in the study of prophecy.

(15) H. H. Rowley: " The Nature of Prophecy in the Light of Recent Study ", in *The Servant of the Lord*, 2nd edn, Blackwell, Oxford, 1965, pp. 97-134. An acutely argued discussion with detailed documentation, of which a simpler version may be found in (15a) Rowley's *The Rediscovery of the Old Testament*, James Clarke, London, 1946, ch. 6, " The Significance of Prophecy ".

(16) O. Eissfeldt: " The Prophetic Literature ", in *The Old Testament and Modern Study*, ed. by H. H. Rowley, Clarendon Press, Oxford, 1951, pp. 115-61. A critical survey of the main scholarly developments, 1935-50.

(17) W. McKane: " Prophecy and the Prophetic Literature ", in *Tradition and Interpretation*, ed. by G. W. Anderson, Clarendon Press, Oxford, 1979, pp. 163-88. A survey of scholarship, 1950-74.

The following volumes contain essays of which all or most deal with various aspects of Prophecy:

(18) *Israel's Prophetic Heritage: Essays in Honour of James Muilenburg*, ed. by B. W. Anderson and Walter Harrelson, Harper, New York, 1962.

(18a) E. Hammershaimb: *Some Aspects of Old Testament Prophecy from Isaiah to Malachi*, Rosenkilde & Bagger, Copenhagen, 1966.

(19) N. W. Porteous: *Living the Mystery*, Blackwell, Oxford, 1967.

(20) *Studies in Old Testament Prophecy Presented to Professor Theodore H. Robinson*, ed. by H. H. Rowley, T. & T. Clark, Edinburgh, 1950.

The following two short works provide well-documented discussions of some of the more important ways in which the study of Prophecy has developed since the 2nd edn of the present work (see also no. (17) above):

(21) R. E. Clements: *Prophecy and Covenant*, S.C.M., London, 1965.

(22) R. E. Clements: *Prophecy and Tradition*, Blackwell, 1975.

CHAPTERS I AND II: Ancient Semitic Religion, and The Two Religions of Israel.

The best short modern introduction to ancient Near Eastern religions is:

(23) H. Ringgren: *Religions of the Ancient Near East* (E.Tr.), S.P.C.K., London, 1973.

Most books on Israelite religion include some account of the religions of Israel's neighbours. The best recent works are:

(24) H. Ringgren: *Israelite Religion* (E.Tr.), S.P.C.K., London, 1966.

(25) Th. C. Vriezen: *The Religion of Ancient Israel* (E.Tr.), Lutterworth, London, 1967. Pp. 22-78 deal with the religions of Israel's neighbours.

(26) G. Fohrer: *The History of Israelite Religion* (E.Tr.), S.P.C.K., London, 1973.

Three books by W. F. Albright are specially relevant:

(27) *From the Stone Age to Christianity*, 1940, 2nd edn in Anchor Books, New York, 1957.

(28) *Archaeology and the Religion of Israel*, Johns Hopkins, Baltimore, 1942.

(29) *Yahweh and the Gods of Canaan*, Athlone Press, London, 1968.

For the specifically Canaanite background, see especially:

(30) J. Gray: *The Legacy of Canaan*, Brill, Leiden, 2nd edn, 1965.

CHAPTERS III AND IV: The N'bi'm, and The Canonical Prophets.

It is now generally held that T. H. Robinson's views on prophetic ecstacy were somewhat extreme and that his treatment of different types of prophet was oversimplified. Reference should be made to Rowley (15) and above all to Lindblom (5), Chs 2 and 3. The evidence for cultic prophets is fully presented in:

(31) A. R. Johnson: *The Cultic Prophet in Ancient Israel*, University of Wales Press, Cardiff, 2nd edn, 1962. See also a much larger work by the same author and from the same Press:

(32) A. R. Johnson: *The Cultic Prophet and Israel's Psalmody*, 1979.

(33) S. Mowinckel: *The Psalms in Israel's Worship*, 2 vols, Blackwell, Oxford, 1962, vol. 2, pp. 53-73.

(34) A. C. Welch: *Prophet and Priest in Old Israel*, 1936; reprint, Blackwell, Oxford, 1953.

(35) N. W. Porteous: " Prophet and Priest in Israel ", in *Expository Times*, lxii, 1950/51, pp. 4-9.

(36) H. H. Rowley: " Ritual and the Hebrew Prophets ", in *Myth, Ritual, and Kingship*, ed. by S. H. Hooke, Clarendon Press, Oxford, 1958, pp. 236-260.

(37) H. H. Rowley: *Worship in Ancient Israel*, S.P.C.K., London, pp. 144-175.

The following two works are valuable for their range and stimulus, but should be read with critical caution:

(38) I. Engnell: " Prophets and Prophetism in the Old Testament ", in *Critical Essays on the Old Testament*, S.P.C.K., London, 1970.

(39) A. Haldar: *Associations of Cult Prophets among the Ancient Semites*, Almqvist & Wiksell, Uppsala, 1945.

CHAPTER V: The Structure of the Prophetic Books.

In addition to the relevant sections of recent Introductions to the Old Testament and commentaries on prophetic books, see the following:

Lindblom (5), Ch. 4; a full and balanced treatment.

(40) S. Mowinckel: *Prophecy and Tradition*, Dybwad, Oslo, 1946.

(41) G. Widengren: *Literary and Psychological Aspects of the Hebrew Prophets*, Lundequistska Bokhandeln, Uppsala, 1948. With this work and no. (40), compare Engnell, no. (38), pp. 163-79.

(42) E. Nielsen: *Oral Tradition*, S.C.M., London, 1954.

(43) C. Westermann: *Basic Forms of Prophetic Speech* (E.Tr.), Lutterworth, London, 1967. A work of exceptional importance.

Valuable critical surveys of work in this field will be found in Eissfeldt (16) and McKane (17), and in:

(44) W. E. March: " Prophecy ", in *Old Testament Form Criticism*, ed. by J. H. Hayes, Trinity U.P., San Antonio, 1974, pp. 141-77.

The items listed below on individual prophetic books and parts of books are classified as (A) = commentaries, and (B) = other studies. They should be supplemented by reference to the relevant sections of the general works on Prophecy mentioned above.

With three notable exceptions, no separate references are made below to commentaries on prophetic books in the following, though they are often well worth consulting for brief expositions:

(45) *The Interpreter's Bible*, vols 5 & 6, Abingdon Press, Nashville, 1956.

(46) *The Jerome Biblical Commentary*, Chapman, London, 1969.

(47) *A New Catholic Commentary on Holy Scripture*, Nelson, London, 1969.

(48) *Peake's Commentary on the Bible*, new edn, Nelson, 1962.

The following, to which no further reference is made below, should also be noted:

(49) J. A. Bewer: *The Prophets in the King James Version with Introduction and Critical Notes*, Eyre and Spottiswoode, London, 1957.

(50) *The Soncino Bible* series, general editor A. Cohen, Soncino Press, London, Hindhead, & Bournemouth: vols on *Isaiah*, 1949; *Jeremiah*, 1949; *Ezekiel*, 1950; *The Twelve Prophets*, 1948. Hebrew text, English translation, short introductions, and concise, practical, Jewish introductions.

Of lasting value are:

(51) G. A. Smith: *The Book of Isaiah*, 2 vols, Hodder & Stoughton, London; last revised edn, 1928.

(52) G. A. Smith: *The Book of the Twelve Prophets*, 2 vols, Hodder & Stoughton, London, last revised edn, 1928.

Originally published in The Expositor's Bible series, these volumes are primarily expository (especially those on Isaiah), but based on sound critical method. Though they are now somewhat dated on various points of scholarship, their outstanding merits remain.

In the lists of commentaries below, the following abbreviations are used:

AB: Anchor Bible, Doubleday, New York. Fairly full, but not severely technical.

CB: Cambridge Bible for Schools and Colleges, Cambridge U.P., Exegetical commentaries on RV (earlier edns on AV).

CBC: Cambridge Bible Commentary. Brief; up-to-date; based on NEB.

CeB: Century Bible, T.C. & E.C. Jack, Edinburgh. Concise; based on RV.

EB: Expositor's Bible, Hodder & Stoughton, London.

IB: Interpreter's Bible. See (45) above. Based on AV and RSV; includes both exegesis and exposition; only exegesis is relevant.

ICC: International Critical Commentary, T. & T. Clark, Edinburgh. Detailed, technical scholarship. Most vols now rather old; but a new series is under preparation.

NCeB: New Century Bible, formerly Nelson, now Oliphants, London. Based on RSV.

OTL: Old Testament Library, S.C.M., London. Independent translations; commentaries contain much original work.

TC: Torch Commentary, S.C.M., London. Based variously on AV and RSV. Short and non-technical.

TyC: Tyndale Old Testament Commentaries, Tyndale Press, London. A moderately conservative series in which the emphasis is on exegesis.

WestC: Westminster Commentaries. A fairly full exegetical series, based on RV.

In addition to the general works mentioned below under the several chapters, it is essential to study the historical background of the work and message of the various prophets as presented in the standard histories of Ancient Israel. Of these the best detailed treatments are:

(53) J. Bright: *A History of Israel,* revised edn, S.C.M., London, 1972.

(54) M. Noth: *The History of Israel* (E.Tr.), 2nd edn, A. & C. Black, London, 1960.

(55) S. Herrmann: *A History of Israel in Old Testament Times* (E.Tr.), S.C.M., London, 1975.

CHAPTER VI: Amos.

(A) (56) S. R. Driver: CB, 2nd edn, rev. by H. C. O. Lanchester, 1915.

(57) H. McKeating: CBC, 1971.

(58) W. R. Harper: ICC, 1905.

(59) J. L. Mays: OTL, 1969.

(60) J. Marsh: TC, 1959.

(61) R. S. Cripps: *A Critical and Exegetical Commentary on the Book of Amos,* 2nd edn, S.P.C.K., London, 1955. A full exegetical commentary on RV.

(62) E. Hammershaimb: *The Book of Amos: A Commentary* (E.Tr.), Blackwell, Oxford, 1970. Based on the Hebrew text; useful for students.

(63) N. H. Snaith: *Notes on the Hebrew Text of Amos,* 2 vols, Epworth Press, London, 1945. A practical textbook.

(64) H. W. Wolff: *Joel and Amos* (E.Tr.), Hermeneia, Fortress Press, Philadelphia, 1977.

Also (52), vol. 1, chs 5-11.

(B) (65) A. S. Kapelrud: *Central Ideas in Amos,* University Press, Oslo, 1961.

(66) J. Morgenstern: *Amos Studies I-III,* Hebrew Union College Press, Cincinnati, 1941.

(67) J. M. Ward: *Amos and Isaiah: Prophets of the Word of God,* Abingdon Press, Nashville, 1969.

(68) J. D. W. Watts: *Vision and Prophecy in Amos,* Baptist Theol. Sem., Ruschlikon/Zurich, 1958.

CHAPTER VII: Hosea.

(A) H. McKeating: CBC, as (57).

W. R. Harper: ICC, as (58).

(69) J. L. Mays: OTL, 1969.

(70) G. A. F. Knight: TC, 1960.

(72) J. M. Ward: *Hosea: A Theological Commentary*, Harper & Row, New York, 1966.

Also (52), vol. 1, chs 12-23.

(B) (72) W. Brueggemann: *Tradition for Crisis*, John Knox Press, Richmond, Va., 1968.

(73) M. J. Buss: *The Prophetic Word of Hosea*, Topelmann, Berlin, 1969. A technical, analytical study.

(74) H. W. Robinson: " The Cross of Hosea ", in *Two Hebrew Prophets*, Lutterworth Press, London, 1948, pp. 11-61.

(75) H. H. Rowley: " The Marriage of Hosea ", in *Men of God*, Nelson, Edinburgh, 1963, pp. 68-97. An acutely argued study, with full references to the relevant literature.

(76) N. H. Snaith: *Mercy and Sacrifice*, S.C.M., London, 1963.

CHAPTER VIII: Judacan Prophets of the Eighth Century: Micah and Isaiah.

(A) *Micah*

H. McKeating: CBC, as (57).

(77) J. M. P. Smith: ICC, 1911.

J. Marsh: TC, as (60).

Also (52), vol. 1, chs 24-31.

Isaiah

(78) J. Skinner: CB, vol. 1, 2nd edn, 1915. This, with vol. 2 on xl-lxvi, is one of the best exegetical commentaries in English on any book of the Old Testament.

(79) A. S. Herbert: CBC, 1973.

(80) O. C. Whitehouse: CeB, vol. 1, 1905.

(81) R. B. Y. Scott: IB, vol. 5, pp. 151-381.

(82) G. B. Gray: ICC, 1912. Only ixxxvii. A superb technical commentary.

(83) O. Kaiser: OTL (E.Tr.), 2 vols – i-xii, 2nd edn, 1972; xiii-xxxix, 1973.

(84) J. Mauchline: TC, 1962.

(85) G. W. Wade: WestC, 2nd edn, 1929.

(86) E. J. Kissane: *The Book of Isaiah*, vol. 1, Browne & Nolan, Dublin, revised edn, 1960.

Also (51), vol. 1.

(B) (87) S. H. Blank: *Prophetic Faith in Isaiah*, A. & C. Black, London, 1958. A stimulating book which departs at many points from generally accepted views.

(88) B. S. Childs: *Isaiah and the Assyrian Crisis*, S.C.M., London, 1967.

Also (67).

CHAPTER IX: The Seventh Century Prophets.
(A) *Zephaniah, Nahum, and Habakkuk*

(89) A. B. Davidson: CB, edn, revised by H. C. O. Lanchester, 1920.

(90) S. R. Driver: CeB, *Minor Prophets*, vol. 2, 1906.

(91) J. M. P. Smith (Zeph. & Nah.) and W. H. Ward (Hab.): ICC, 1911.

Also (52) vol. 2, chs 1-12.

(B) (92) A. Haldar: *Studies in the Book of Nahum*, Uppsala, 1947.

CHAPTER X: Jeremiah.
(A) (93) J. Bright: AB, 1965.

(94) A. W. Streane: CB, 2nd edn, 1913.

(95) E. W. Nicholson: CBC, 2 vols, 1973, 1975.

(96) A. S. Peake: CeB, 2 vols, 1910, 1912.

(97) H. Cunliffe-Jones: TC, 2nd edn, 1966.

(98) R. K. Harrison: TyC, 1973.

(99) L. E. Binns: WestC, 1919.

(100) S. R. Driver: *The Book of the Prophet Jeremiah: A Revised Translation with Introductions and Short Explanations*, Hodder & Stoughton, London, 1906. Admirably concise.

(101) E. A. Leslie: *Jeremiah Chronologically Arranged, translated, and Interpreted*, Abingdon Press, Nashville, 1954.

(B) (102) P. R. Ackroyd: *Exile and Restoration: A Study of Hebrew Thought of the Sixth Century B. C.*, S.C.M., London, 1968. This book is of great importance for the Prophets from Jeremiah to Zechariah. For Jeremiah, see Chapter IV.

(103) E. W. Nicholson: *Preaching to the Exiles: A Study of the Prose Tradition in Jeremiah*, Blackwell, 1970.

(104) H. W. Robinson: " The Cross of Jeremiah ", in *The Cross in the Old Testament*, S.C.M., London, 1955, pp. 115-92.

(105) H. H. Rowley: " The Early Prophecies of Jeremiah in their Setting ", in *Men of God*, Nelson, Edinburgh, 1963, pp. 133-68.

(106) H. H. Rowley: " The Prophet Jaremiah and the Book of Deuteronomy ", in *From Moses to Qumran*, Lutterworth, London, 1963, pp. 187-208.

(107) J. Skinner: *Prophecy and Religion*, Cambridge, 1922. A masterly interpretation of Jeremiah's teaching and of his place in the development of Israel's religion.

(108) A. C. Welch: *Jeremiah: His Time and His Work*, 1928; reprinted, Blackwell, Oxford, 1951.

CHAPTER XI: The Exile: Ezekiel.

(A) (109) A. B. Davidson: CB, 1893, 2nd edn, revised by A. W. Streane, 1916. A first-rate exegetical commentary.

(110) K. W. Carley: CBC, 1974.

(111) W. F. Lofthouse: CeB, 1909. A masterpiece of compression and clarity.

(112) J. Skinner: EB, 1895.

(113) H. G. May: IB, vol. 6, pp. 41-338; see (45).

(114) G. A. Cooke: ICC, 1936.

(115) J. W. Wevers: NCeB, 1969.

(116) W. Eichrodt: OTL, 1970

(117) D. M. G. Stalker: TC, 1968.

(118) J. B. Taylor, TyC, 1969.

(B) (119) H. L. Ellison: *Ezekiel: The Man and His Message*, Paternoster Press, London, 1956.

(120) J. B. Harford: *Studies in the Book of Ezekiel*, Cambridge, 1935. Includes a valuable critical survey of scholarship up to 1932.

(121) W. F. Lofthouse: *The Prophet of Reconstruction: A Patriot's Ideal for a New Age*, James Clarke, London, 1920.

(122) H. W. Robinson: " The Visions of Ezekiel ", in *Two Hebrew Prophets*, pp. 65-125; cf. (74).

(123) H. H. Rowley: " The Book of Ezekiel in Modern Study ", in *Men of God*, pp. 169-210; cf. (105).

See also (102), Chapter VII.

Though this bibliography is confined to books and articles in English, it would be inappropriate if no mention were made of the contributions made to the study of Ezekiel by W. Zimmerli, above all in his massive commentary in the *Biblischer Kommentar* series, 2 vols, Neukirchen, 1969, of which an English translation is in preparation. For a brief sample of Zimmerli's work, see " The Special Form-and Traditio-historical character of Ezekiel's prophecy ", in *Vetus Testamentum*, XV, 1965, pp. 515-27.

CHAPTERS XII & XIII: The Prophets of the Return, and Prophecy in the Restored Community.

(A) *Isaiah xl-lxvi*

(124) J. L. McKenzie: AB, 1968. Includes xxxiv, xxxv, xl-lxvi.

(125) J. Skinner: CB, vol. 2, 2nd edn 1917; cf. (78).

(126) A. S. Herbert: CBC, 1975.

(127) O. C. Whitehouse: CeB, vol. 2, 1908; cf. (80).

(128) J. Muilenburg: IB, vol. 5, pp. 381-773; see (45).

(129) C. Westermann: OTL, 1969.

(130) C. R. North: TC, Isaiah xl-lv, 1952.

(131) D. R. Jones: TC, Isaiah ixi-lxvi, and Joel, 1964.

G. W. Wade: WestC, as (85).

(132) E. J. Kissane: vol. 2, 1943; cf. (86).

(133) R. Levy: *Deutero-Isaiah: A Commentary*, Oxford University Press, 1925. An admirably concise commentary on xl-lv. Discusses Det.-Isa.'s influence on Jewish thought.

(134) C. R. North: *The Second Isaiah: Introduction, Translation and Commentary to Chapters XL-LV*, Clarendon Press, Oxford, 1963.

(135) U. E. Simon: *A Theology of Salvation: A Commentary on Isaiah 40-55*, S.P.C.K., London, 1953.

(136) J. D. Smart: *History and Theology in Second Isaiah: A Commentary on Isaiah 35, 40-66*, Epworth Press, London, 1965. Diverges at important points from general accepted views.

Also (51), vol. 2.

(B) *General Studies on Isaiah xl-lxvi*

(137) S. Smith: *Isaiah Chapters XL-LV: Literary Criticism and History*, Oxford University Press, London, 1944. Schweich Lectures.

(138) C. R. North: *The Suffering Servant in Deutero-Isaiah*, Oxford University Press, London, 2nd edn, 1946. Presents in detail the history of scholarship and the arguments for the author's own view. A model of exact scholarship.

(139) H. M. Orlinsky & N. H. Snaith: *Studies on the Second Part of the Book of Isaiah*, Brill, Leiden, 1967. Two quite separate studies presenting independent views.

(140) A. S. Peake: *The Servant of Yahweh*, Manchester University Press, 1931, pp. 1-74.

(141) H. W. Robinson: " The Cross of the Servant ", in *The Cross in the Old Testament*, pp. 55-114; cf. (104).

(142) H. H. Rowley: " The Servant of the Lord in the Light of Three Decades of Criticism ", in *The Servant of the Lord*; pp. 1-60; cf. (15).

(143) H. H. Rowley: " The Suffering Servant and the Davidic Messiah ", op. cit., pp. 61-93.

Also (102), Chapter VIII.

(A) *Haggai, Zechariah, Malachi, Jonah*

(144) W. E. Barnes: CB, 1917 (Hag., Zech., Mal.).

(145) H. C. O. Lanchester: CB, 1915 (Obad., & Jonah).

(146) R. Mason: CBC, 1977 (Hag., Zech., Mal.).

(147) H. G. Mitchell, J. M. P. Smith, and J. A. Bewer: ICC, 1912.

(148) Joyce G. Baldwin: TyC, 1972 (Hag., Zech., Mal.).

Also (52) vol. 2, chs 17-26, 34-8; and (90).

(B) (102), chs 9-11.

Chapter XIV: Eschatology.

(A) *Isaiah xxiv-xxvii*
See the commentaries on Isaiah i-xxxix, under Chapter VIII, above.

Joel

S. R. Driver: CB, as (56).

J. A. Bewer: ICC, as (77).

Also (52), vol. 2, chs 27-30; (131).

(B) *On Joel*

(149) A. S. Kapelrud: *Joel Studies*, Uppsala, 1948.

On the Messianic Hope, Eschatology, and Apocalyptic

(150) A. Bentzen: *King and Messiah* (E.Tr.), 2nd edn, Blackwell, Oxford, 1970.

(151) P. D. Hanson: *The Dawn of Apocalyptic: The Historical and Sociological Roots of Jewish Apocalyptic Eschatology*, Fortress Press, Philadelphia, 1975.

(152) J. Klausner: *The Messianic Idea in Israel* (E.Tr.), Allen & Unwin, London, 1955.

(153) S. Mowinckel: *He That Cometh* (E.Tr.), Blackwell, Oxford, 1956.

(154) E. W. Nicholson: " Apocalyptic ", in *Tradition and Interpretation*, pp. 189-213; cf. (17).

(155) A. S. Peake: " The Roots of Hebrew Prophecy and Jewish Apocalyptic ", in *The Servant of Yahweh*, pp. 75-110; cf. (140).

(156) O. Ploger: *Theocracy and Eschatology* (E.Tr.), Blackwell, Oxford, 1968.

(157) H. Ringgren: *The Messiah in the Old Testament* (E.Tr.), S.C.M., London, 1956.

(158) H. H. Rowley: *The Relevance of Apocalyptic*, 3rd edn, Lutterworth Press, London, 1963.

(159) D. S. Russell: *The Method and Message of Jewish Apocalyptic*, S.C.M., London, 1964.

Also (4), pp. 301-15; and (143).

ADDENDA

Professor Robinson nowhere discusses in any detail the importance of Elijah. The following two essays are of great value, both for their content and for their documentation:

(160) A. S. Peake: " Elijah and Jezebel: The Conflict with the Tyrian Baal ", in *The Servant of Yahweh*, pp. 111-50; cf. (140).

(161) H. H. Rowley: " Elijah on Mount Carmel ", in *Men of God*, pp. 37-65; cf. (105).

The following work deals comprehensively with the bearing of the prophetic teaching on international relations in the ancient Near East:

(162) N. K. Gottwald: *All the Kingdoms of the Earth*, Harper & Row, New York, 1964.